AFRICAN COOKERY

A
Black
Heritage

by
Annette Merson

Winston-Derek Publishers, Inc.
Pennywell Drive—Post Office Box 90883
Nashville, Tennessee 37209

Copyright 1987 by Winston-Derek Publishers, Inc.

All rights reserved. No part of this book may be reproduced in any form without written permission from the publishers, except by a reviewer who may quote brief passages in a review to be printed in a newspaper or magazine.

First printing

```
TX
725
.A4
M45
1987
```

PUBLISHED BY WINSTON-DEREK PUBLISHERS, INC.
Nashville, Tennessee 37205

Library of Congress Catalogue Card No: 86-40283
ISBN 1-55523-027-X

Printed in the United States of America

CONTENTS

The Significance of the Geometric Designs of This Book v
Food and Its importance in Africa Past and Present vi
Of Interest Regarding Food and Drink in America vii

SAUCES
    Berberé 1
    Niter Kebbeh 2
    Berber and Tainey 3

APPETIZERS AND SOUPS
    Kitfo 4
    Samosas 5
    Avocado Smoked Fish 6
    Fish-Shrimp Salad 7
    Supu Ya N Dizi 8
    Curry-Beef Soup 9
    Snyssels Milk Soup 10
    Papaya Soup 11

MAIN DISHES
    African Almond Chicken 12
    Doro Wat 13
    African Chicken Pie 14
    African Chicken and Greens 15
    Chicken-Goober Stew 16
    Dried Fruit Curry 17
    Sosaties 18
    Bootjiebredie 19
    Bobotie 20
    Frikkadels 22
    Mock Venison 23
    Afrikander 24
    Segana Dora Wat 25
    Meat Lagos 26
    Zanzibar 27
    Gesmoorde Vis 28
    Ingelegde Vis 29
    Wali Na Samaki 30
    Yoruba 31
    Peixe a Lumbo 32

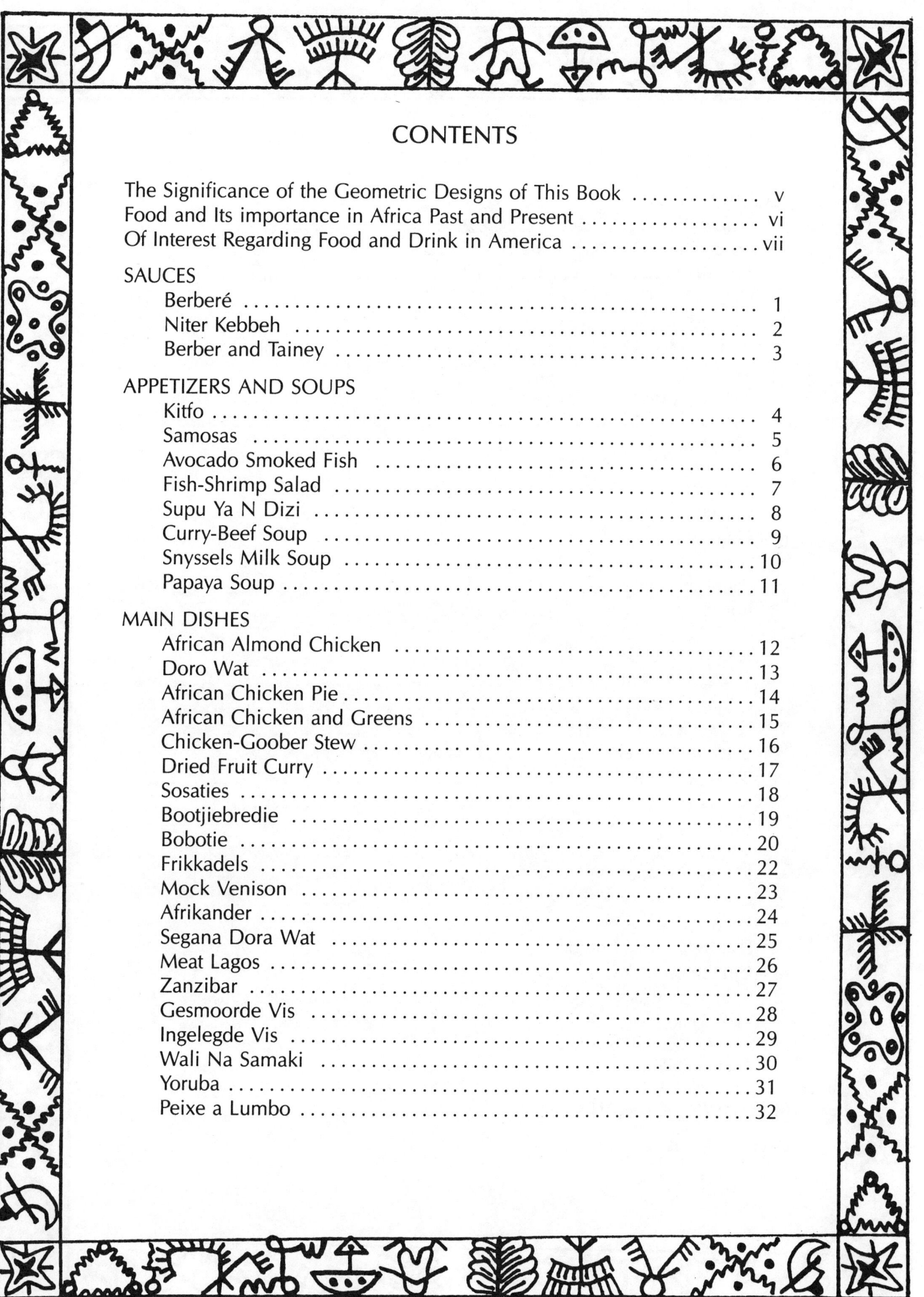

    Couscous 33
    Nigerian Crabs and Rice 34

VEGETABLES
    Spicy Okra 35
    Spicy Diced Tomato Salad 36
    Red Beet and Onion Salad 36
    Cucumber-Chili Salad 37
    Avocado-Ginger Salad 37
    Green Bean Atjar 38
    Yams 39
    Fufu Dumplings 40
    Yam or Sweet Potato Stew 41
    Yataklete Kilkil 42

SIDE DISHES
    Governor's Beans 43
    Geelrys 44
    Arroz de Coco 45
    Yemiser Salatta 46
    Injera 47

DESSERTS
    Tanzanian Fruit Salad 48
    Steamed Papaya 49
    Ovos Moles De Papaia 50
    Cocada Amarela 51
    Banana Fritters 52
    Koeksisters 53
    Krakelinge 54
    Soetkoekies 55
    Ginger Cookies 56
    Coconut Lemon Cookies 57
    Peanut Cookies 58
    Plantain Gingerbread 59
    Cinnamon Cake 60
    Cornmeal Cake 61
    Pineapple Pie 62

SUGGESTIONS 63

ACKNOWLEDGEMENTS 68

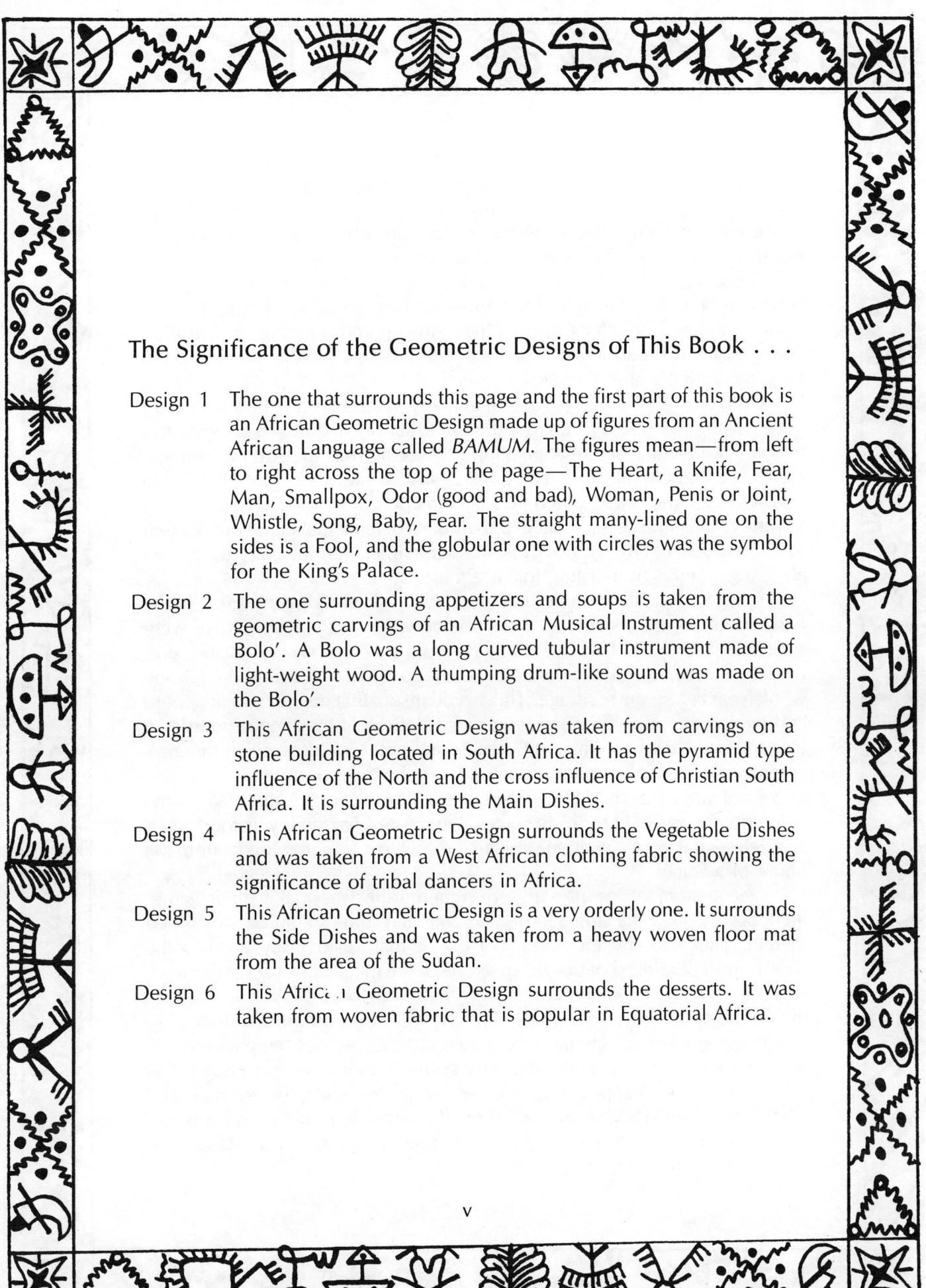

The Significance of the Geometric Designs of This Book...

Design 1 The one that surrounds this page and the first part of this book is an African Geometric Design made up of figures from an Ancient African Language called *BAMUM*. The figures mean—from left to right across the top of the page—The Heart, a Knife, Fear, Man, Smallpox, Odor (good and bad), Woman, Penis or Joint, Whistle, Song, Baby, Fear. The straight many-lined one on the sides is a Fool, and the globular one with circles was the symbol for the King's Palace.

Design 2 The one surrounding appetizers and soups is taken from the geometric carvings of an African Musical Instrument called a Bolo'. A Bolo was a long curved tubular instrument made of light-weight wood. A thumping drum-like sound was made on the Bolo'.

Design 3 This African Geometric Design was taken from carvings on a stone building located in South Africa. It has the pyramid type influence of the North and the cross influence of Christian South Africa. It is surrounding the Main Dishes.

Design 4 This African Geometric Design surrounds the Vegetable Dishes and was taken from a West African clothing fabric showing the significance of tribal dancers in Africa.

Design 5 This African Geometric Design is a very orderly one. It surrounds the Side Dishes and was taken from a heavy woven floor mat from the area of the Sudan.

Design 6 This African Geometric Design surrounds the desserts. It was taken from woven fabric that is popular in Equatorial Africa.

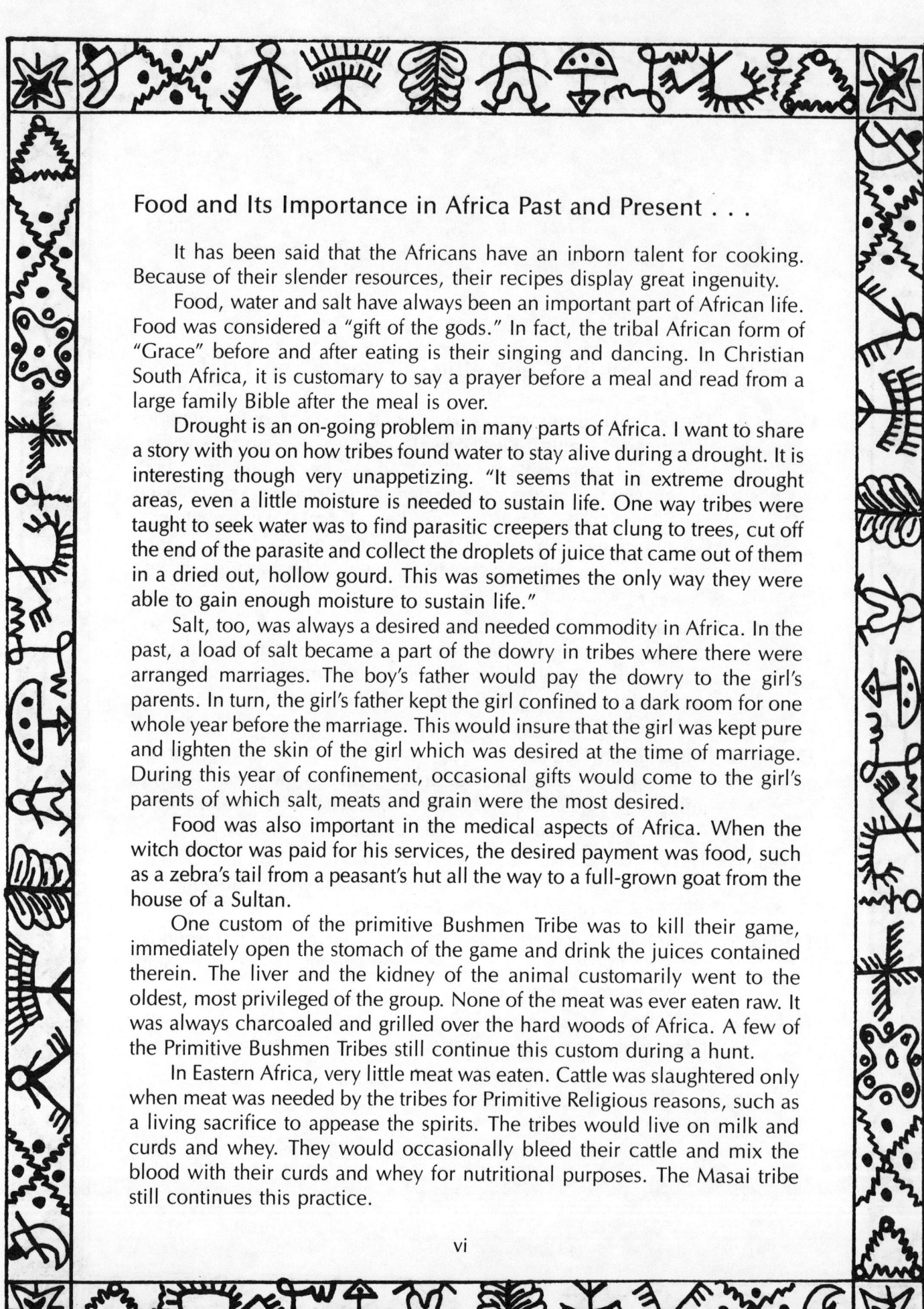

Food and Its Importance in Africa Past and Present . . .

It has been said that the Africans have an inborn talent for cooking. Because of their slender resources, their recipes display great ingenuity.

Food, water and salt have always been an important part of African life. Food was considered a "gift of the gods." In fact, the tribal African form of "Grace" before and after eating is their singing and dancing. In Christian South Africa, it is customary to say a prayer before a meal and read from a large family Bible after the meal is over.

Drought is an on-going problem in many parts of Africa. I want to share a story with you on how tribes found water to stay alive during a drought. It is interesting though very unappetizing. "It seems that in extreme drought areas, even a little moisture is needed to sustain life. One way tribes were taught to seek water was to find parasitic creepers that clung to trees, cut off the end of the parasite and collect the droplets of juice that came out of them in a dried out, hollow gourd. This was sometimes the only way they were able to gain enough moisture to sustain life."

Salt, too, was always a desired and needed commodity in Africa. In the past, a load of salt became a part of the dowry in tribes where there were arranged marriages. The boy's father would pay the dowry to the girl's parents. In turn, the girl's father kept the girl confined to a dark room for one whole year before the marriage. This would insure that the girl was kept pure and lighten the skin of the girl which was desired at the time of marriage. During this year of confinement, occasional gifts would come to the girl's parents of which salt, meats and grain were the most desired.

Food was also important in the medical aspects of Africa. When the witch doctor was paid for his services, the desired payment was food, such as a zebra's tail from a peasant's hut all the way to a full-grown goat from the house of a Sultan.

One custom of the primitive Bushmen Tribe was to kill their game, immediately open the stomach of the game and drink the juices contained therein. The liver and the kidney of the animal customarily went to the oldest, most privileged of the group. None of the meat was ever eaten raw. It was always charcoaled and grilled over the hard woods of Africa. A few of the Primitive Bushmen Tribes still continue this custom during a hunt.

In Eastern Africa, very little meat was eaten. Cattle was slaughtered only when meat was needed by the tribes for Primitive Religious reasons, such as a living sacrifice to appease the spirits. The tribes would live on milk and curds and whey. They would occasionally bleed their cattle and mix the blood with their curds and whey for nutritional purposes. The Masai tribe still continues this practice.

In fact, some primitive tribes believed that their cattle were sacred, and that one's ancestors could talk to them through the sounds that the cattle made.

There were many tribal differences in the eating of other animals such as zebras, antelopes, hippos, elephants, etc. What may be food for one tribe, may be taboo for another tribe. Taboos still affect many tribes in Africa today.

Still today, in many parts of Africa, one main meal is eaten. The rest of the day, people snack on dried meats, damp roasted barley and curds and whey.

Of Interest Regarding Food and Drink in Africa . . .

It is an Ethiopian claim that coffee originated in their country and came from a place called Kaffa. The Africans make a very heavy, strong coffee, sweetened with sugar or wild honey. It is interesting to note here that all villages have their prized honey trees.

Thalla was the very first alcoholic drink of Africa. It basically is a poor man's beer made from millet fermented in clay vats.

Tedj is an African Liquor. It was the first alcoholic drink of the classical era. When Tedj is served at the end of a dry day of travel, it warms the body and quenches the thirst. It can be served in earthenware with a covering of leaves.

Wild game such as gazelles, elephants, hippos, warthogs, zebras and camels are also eaten in Africa. Many of these meats are ground or minced for tenderizing purposes.

Gazelles are cut into fillets, roasted over hard woods and served with red currant jelly, red cabbage and wild honey.

Hippo is known for the finest "natural" lard in the world. The giraffe's marrow was "the delicacy of primitive man," and the warthog is the counterpart of our boars.

The *YAM* is the "Native Staple" of Africa. It is part of many celebrations and Yam Feast Days.

And last of all, fruits and spices grown in various parts of Africa are very important to African Cookery and the Africans' Diet.

And now, the recipes . . . try and enjoy an experience in Black Heritage cooking.

SPICES are an integral part of African Cookery as you shall see by the various spices used in the recipes in this book. I am not only talking about "hot spicy tangy" but also just about foods that are highly enhanced by that special touch of certain spices. African Cookery will provide a venture for your tastebuds and an "aromatic experience."

Spices you may want to use in *AFRICAN COOKERY*—

- Allspice (Ground and Whole)
- Basil
- Bay Leaves
- Black Pepper (Ground)
- Cardamon (Ground and Pods)
- Carraway Seeds
- Cayenne Pepper
- Cinnamon (Ground and Stick)
- Cloves (Ground and Whole)
- Coriander (Ground)
- Curry Powder
- Dry Mustard
- Fenugreek Seeds
- Ginger (Ground and Fresh Root)
- Mace
- Marjoram
- Mint
- Nutmeg
- Paprika
- Red Pepper (Flakes and Ground)
- Salt
- Savory Spice
- Thyme
- Turmeric
- White Pepper (Ground)

MANY, many spices are grown in Africa and they are widely used to highly enhance the delicious recipes!

Hint: Buy spices at an import store that sells them in bulk by the ounce or half-ounce.

Sauces

Berberé (Bāir bāir ā)

A *SPICE PASTE* that originated in Ethiopia, Berberé is the official language of Ethiopia as well as the name for this fiery pepper sauce. Tribal customs dictated that this sauce be used with warm fresh raw meat dishes. It is definitely hot enough to give the impression that the meat was cooked. It is also used as a coating in the drying of meats. You will find it always at hand in an Ethiopian kitchen. It is used in some recipes and otherwise may be served along with other recipes. This recipe makes two cups and may be stored safely in the refrigerator for up to 6 months.

1 tsp. ground Ginger
½ tsp. ground Cardamon
½ tsp. ground Coriander
½ tsp. Fenugreek Seeds
¼ tsp. ground Nutmeg
⅛ tsp. ground Cloves
⅛ tsp. ground Cinnamon
⅛ tsp. ground Allspice
2 tbls. Onions (chop finely)

1 tbls. Garlic (chop finely)
2 tbls. Salt
3 tbls. Dry Red Wine
2 cups Paprika
2 tbls. Red Pepper (flakes)
½ tsp. Black Pepper
1½ cups Water
2 tbls. Vegetable Oil

In a large non-stick frying pan or 3 quart non-stick saucepan, toast the following spices at medium heat for 1 minute: ginger, cardamon, coriander, fenugreek seeds, nutmeg, cloves, cinnamon, and allspice. Stir constantly. This will enhance the flavor of the spices. Then, remove the pan from the heat and let it cool for 10 minutes.

Place the toasted spices in a blender along with the finely chopped onions and garlic. Also add the salt and wine. Blend all at high speed until it forms a smooth paste. Next, place 2 cups paprika, red pepper flakes and black pepper in a non-stick pan and toast at medium heat for 1 minute stirring constantly. Then add ¼ cup of water at a time until the whole 1½ cups of water are stirred in. Next stir in the 2 tbls. of vegetable oil. Last, add the wine-spice mixture from the blender. Cook over low heat for 15 minutes, stirring constantly. Place Berberé in a jar or crock, cover and refrigerate. Stores in the refrigerator for up to 6 months.

SAUCES

Niter Kebbeh (Nē tāir Kā bā)

A SPICY BUTTER OIL that originated in Ethiopia. This is usually found stored in earthenware in an Ethiopian kitchen and used often. This recipe makes two cups and may be stored safely in the refrigerator for up to six (6) months.

- 2 lbs. unsalted Butter (cut into small pieces)
- 1 small chopped Onion
- 3 tbls. chopped Garlic
- 4 tsp. Ginger (ground and grated Fresh Ginger Root)
- 1½ tsp. Turmeric
- 1 Cardamon Pod (crushed)
- 1 Stick Cinnamon
- 1 tsp. Cloves (ground)
- ⅛ tsp. Nutmeg

Melt the butter in a heavy 4-quart saucepan over medium heat. *Do Not* let it brown. Increase the heat and bring the butter to a boil. Stir in onion, garlic and all spices. Lower heat to low or simmer and cook mixture for 45 minutes uncovered. Stir frequently. Then pour mixture into a jar through a sieve that is lined with 4 layers of cheesecloth. If any spices or solids are left in the oil, strain it again and again until the oil is clear. Throw away spices and solids. If solids are left in the oil, it will not store well and will become rancid quickly. Place oil in a jar, cover and store in the refrigerator for up to 6 months.

SAUCES

Berber and Tainey (Bār bār)

A SAUCE FOR CHICKEN OR BARBEQUED MEATS . . . originated in North Africa and makes 1 cup. The name Berber in this recipe was the name of a North African Tribe who were considered barbarians and were known for their great skill as horsemen.

5 tbls. soft Butter	Pinch of chopped Mint
⅔ cup Peanut Oil	1 tsp. Honey
1½ tsp. Curry Powder	Juice of 1 Lemon
¼ tsp. Red Pepper Flakes	¼ tsp. Basil
1 tbls. ground Peanuts	¼ tsp. Marjoram
1 heaping tbls. Raisins	¼ tsp. Allspice

Soak raisins in lemon juice for 15 minutes. Then add butter, peanut oil, curry, red pepper, peanuts, mint, honey, basil, marjoram and allspice to the bowl and mix well. It is now ready to be used as a barbeque or basting sauce for chicken and other meats.

Appetizers and Soups

Kitfo (Kēy fō)

RAW BEEF AND SPICES . . . this recipe originated in Ethiopia and serves six (6). This dish is an Ethiopian favorite.

- ¼ cup Niter Kebbeh
- ½ cup Onions (chop finely)
- 4 tbls. Green Pepper (chop finely)
- 2 tbls. Chilies (chop finely)
- 1 tsp. Ginger (ground)
- ½ tsp. Garlic (chop finely)
- ½ tsp. Cardamon (ground)
- 1 tbls. Lemon Juice
- 2 tsp. Berberé Sauce
- 2 tsp. Salt
- 2 lbs. Ground Round Steak

In a large skillet, melt the Niter Kebbeh over low heat. Add onions, green pepper, chilies, ginger, garlic and cardamon. Raise heat to medium and cook 2 minutes, stirring constantly. Place mixture in a bowl and cool for 15 minutes. Stir in lemon juice, Berberé and salt. Stir in raw beef and mix thoroughly. Serve with Injera, Breads, or Crackers. Kitfo can also be stuffed in split Italian Frying Peppers and served in this fashion.

APPETIZERS AND SOUPS

Samosas

SPICED MEATY PASTRY . . . this recipe originated in South Africa and serves eight (8). This dish is likely to be traditionally served at "high tea" in South Africa.

1 lb. Ground Beef	¼ tsp. Cayenne Pepper
3 Red Bell Peppers (chop)	5 Cardemon pods (crushed)
6 cloves Garlic (chop finely)	1 tsp. Cinnamon
2 tsp. Carraway Seeds	Juice of 2 Lemons
1 lb. Onions (chop finely)	2 lbs. Flour
Salt and Pepper to taste	Oil for Frying

In a large bowl, place the ground beef and then add chopped red peppers, salt, garlic, carraway, onions, cayenne pepper, cardamon, cinnamon and juice of lemons. Mix well together as you would when making a meatloaf. Take some of the flour and flour a board. Place the meat mixture on the floured surface and knead and mix in one cup of flour at a time until the whole 2 lbs. of flour is kneaded in. Then form meat-dough balls about the size of a small meatball and fry on all sides in oil until browned. Frying time is 10 to 15 minutes per batch. Drain on paper towels and serve warm.

APPETIZERS AND SOUPS

Avocado Smoked Fish

A CONGO AREA tribe known as the Senegalese originated this recipe. It is known as the Seneglese's Quiche.

4 hard-boiled Eggs	½ lb. Smoked Fish
¼ cup Milk	2 large ripe Avocados
¼ cup Lime Juice	1 Red Bell Pepper (cut in strips)
¼ tsp. Sugar	or
⅓ cup Vegetable Oil	1 can Pimentos (cut in strips)
2 tbls. Olive Oil	

　　Peel hard-boiled eggs and take out egg yolks. Mash egg yolks in a large bowl. Mix in the milk and stir until it forms a smooth paste. Add 1 tbls. of the lime juice, the sugar and the salt. Mix well. Pour in the vegetable oil and the olive oil. Then stir in the rest of the lime juice. In a separate bowl, place the chopped egg whites and flaked smoked fish. Make sure all skin and bones are removed. Then add the fish and egg whites to the sauce; toss gently and thoroughly. Refrigerate mixture and then just before serving, cut avocados in half, take out seeds and all the brown fibers. Spoon mixture into avocado halves and top with either red pepper strips or pimento strips. Serve immediately.

Fish-Shrimp Salad

THE SEAS AND RIVERS of Africa are a great source of food. Tribesmen are quite adept at building traps. They are skillful fishermen and will courageously fish and trap even in areas of dangerous rapids. This recipe originated in the Ivory Coast Area of West Africa and serves six (6).

- 1 lb. medium Shrimp (uncooked)
- 1½ lbs. Halibut or Haddock Steaks (1 inch thick)
- 4 cups Water
- 1 cup Onion (chop finely)
- 1 tbls. Salt
- 2 Bay leaves
- 6 Whole Peppercorns

Salad Ingredients:

2 medium tomatoes cooked 15 seconds in boiling water, rinsed in cold water, peeled and diced in a bowl.

- ½ cup Onions (chop finely)
- ¼ cup Red Bell Pepper (chop)
- ½ cup Green Pepper (strips)
- 2 tbls. Parsley (chopped)
- 1 tbls. Chilies (chopped)
- 1 tbls. chopped Garlic
- ⅓ cup Lemon Juice
- ¼ cup Olive Oil
- 2 tbls. Tomato Paste
- ¼ tsp. Black Pepper

Shell and devein shrimp. Wash shrimp in cold water and drain in a colander. Wrap and tie fish in 2 layers of cheesecloth. Set fish and shrimp aside. In a large saucepan place 4 cups water, 1 cup onions, 2 bay leaves, 6 peppercorns and 1 tbls. salt. Bring to a boil over high heat. Reduce heat to simmer and add cheesecloth wrapped fish. Simmer for 5 minutes and then add shrimp and simmer 5 minutes more. With tongs, take out fish and place on one plate. Take out shrimp and place on another plate. Strain the stock into a bowl and throw away the solids. Remove the fish from the cheesecloth, take out any bones, skin and flake fish into a clean bowl. Chop shrimp into ½-inch pieces and place in same bowl. Mix. Then add chopped tomatoes, ½ cup finely chopped onions, red peppers, green peppers, parsley, chilies and garlic. Mix well. In a small bowl, mix together the lemon juice, olive oil, ⅔ cup of leftover stock and the tomato paste and black pepper. Mix well, then pour this sauce over the fish and shrimp salad. Toss gently. Let salad marinate for 30 minutes at room temperature. Serve at room temperature or cold from the refrigerator.

APPETIZERS AND SOUPS

Supu Ya N Dizi (Sūpū Yäh N DēZē)

CHICKEN AND BANANA SOUP—this recipe originated in Tanzania, East Africa and serves six (6).

- 5 lbs. Chicken (cut in pieces)
- 2 quarts Water
- 5 greenish Bananas (quartered)
- 4 large Tomatoes (sliced)
- 3 cups Celery (chopped)
- 1 cup Shredded Coconut
- 1 tbls. Curry Powder
- 1 tbls. Red Pepper
- 1 tbls. Salt
- 1 tsp. Black Pepper
- 8 tbls. Butter
- 1 clove crushed Garlic

Place chicken pieces and water into a large pot. Bring to a boil and boil 5 minutes. Add tomatoes, bananas, celery, coconut, curry, red pepper, salt, black pepper, butter and garlic. Turn down to low heat and simmer (covered) for 30 minutes or until chicken is well done. Serve Hot!

APPETIZERS AND SOUPS

Curry-Beef Soup

THIS ENTICING SOUP recipe originated in South Africa with the curry spice influence of the North and serves six (6).

- 6 cups Beef Stock (Beef Bouillon)
- 1 lb. Beef (cubed)
- 2 Onions (chopped)
- 2 tbls. Curry Powder
- 2 Bay Leaves
- 2 Potatoes (sliced)
- 2 tbls. Vinegar
- 2 tsp. Salt

In a large saucepan or pot, brown the beef cubes and onions in butter. Then add the bouillon, curry and bay leaves. Cook at low heat for 30 minutes. Add the potatoes, vinegar and salt and simmer for 45 minutes to 1 hour until all is tender. Serve Hot!

APPETIZERS AND SOUPS

Snyssels Milk Soup (Snī sěls)

WEST AFRICA is where this recipe is widely used and it serves six (6). The meaning of Synssels is case slicelings of homemade pasta from wheat flour which is boiled in milk. The wonderful aromatic steam of cinnamon fills the air.

    3 cups Milk   ¾ cup Peanut Butter
    3 cups Chicken Bouillon   1 tbls. Minced Onion
    2 tbls. Cornstarch   1 stick Cinnamon

In a large saucepan add the milk slowly to the cornstarch. Stir constantly. Add the rest of the ingredients and simmer for 5 minutes at low heat. Beat with a rotary mixer for 1 minute, strain and serve hot.

(Now, if you want the ultimate in Milk Soup, add the following.)

Mix together 1 cup wheat flour, 1 tsp. salt and 3 eggs. Knead dough until smooth and elastic. Roll out on a floured surface until dough is very thin. Let it dry for 10 minutes. Cut into strips. Flour strips and pile on top of each other. Shread strips into tiny pieces. Separate shredded pieces and boil for 15 minutes in boiling salted water. Drain and rinse in a colander and then add to the Milk Soup and simmer for 10 minutes. Serve Hot!

APPETIZERS AND SOUPS

Papaya Soup

PAPAYA SO CLEAR AND SO LIGHT. This recipe originated in South Africa and serves four (4).

    3 tbls. Butter
    1 medium Onion (sliced thin)
    2 bunches Parsley (chopped)
    1 cup Papaya Juice
    1 large Papaya (seeded, peeled and cubed)
    3 cups Milk
    1 tsp. Salt
    ½ tsp. Pepper
    1 pinch Mace
    1 tbls. Cornstarch

Place butter and onions in a skillet and cook until golden brown over moderate heat. Add Papaya juice, parsley and salt. Then add cubed Papaya and simmer at a low heat until the Papaya becomes a pulp. Press all through a sieve into a large pot. Season with mace and pepper. Stir in the cornstarch with a little water and add it to the soup to thicken it slightly. Then add the milk and simmer for 3 to 5 minutes longer at low heat. Serve hot with croutons.

Main Dishes

African Almond Chicken

THIS RECIPE originated in North Africa near Tripoli and not far from the Gulf of Sidra which is the Almond-growing area of Africa.

3 lbs. Chicken (whole)	½ cup Almonds (chopped)
1 pkg. frozen Peas	1 cup Celery (diced)
2 cups Chicken Stock	Salt to taste
1 tbls. Sherry	3 tbls. Vegetable Oil

Boil chicken in water until tender—about 30 minutes. Take out and set aside to cool. Save 2 cups of the chicken stock. Debone the cooled chicken and cut into 2-inch or smaller pieces. Brown the pieces in 3 tbls. vegetable oil. Then add the celery, peas, chicken stock, almonds, salt and sherry. Simmer 10 minutes. Thicken sauce with 2 tbls. cornstarch mixed in ¼ cup water. Add to sauce and bring to a boil until it thickens. Serve with noodles or a bowl of steaming rice. Serves four (4).

MAIN DISHES/CHICKEN

Doro Wat (Dō rō Wäht)

ALL "WAT" DISHES are considered the "National Dishes" of this part of Africa, namely Ethiopia. A "WAT" dish is to an African what Spaghetti is to an Italian. This recipe is stewed chicken in Red Pepper Sauce and it originated in Ethiopia. Serves four (4).

3 lbs. Chicken (cut in pieces)	¼ tsp. ground Cardamon
3 tbls. Lemon Juice	⅛ tsp. Nutmeg
2 tsp. Salt	¼ cup Berbere'
2 cups Onion (chop finely)	2 tbls. Paprika
1 Tlbs. Butter	¼ cup Dry Red or White Wine
¼ cup Niter Kebbeh	¾ cup Water
1 tsp. Ginger	⅛ tsp. Black Pepper
1 tbls. Garlic (chop finely)	4 Hard-boiled Eggs
¼ tsp. Fenugreek Seeds	

Rub the chicken pieces with the lemon juice and salt and let it set at room temperature for 30 minutes. In a 4-quart dutch oven or saucepan, cook the 2 cups of onions in 1 tbls. butter for 5 to 6 minutes at moderate heat. Add the Niter Kebbeh, garlic, ginger, fenugreek seeds, cardamon, nutmeg, Berbere' and paprika. Cook over low heat 2 to 3 minutes. Add the wine and water. Raise heat to high and bring to a boil. Lower to medium heat and cook 5 minutes until it thickens to a gravy consistency. Add the chicken to the sauce, turn until coated on all sides, cover and simmer at low heat for 15 to 20 minutes. Take the hard-boiled eggs, peel and poke holes all over them with a fork. Add the eggs to the chicken and sauce and cover again. Cook at low heat for 20 more minutes. Sprinkle with pepper and serve. Serve with injera, a bowl of steaming rice or plain yogurt. It is also delicious with Kil Kil (see page 44 under vegetables.)

MAIN DISHES/CHICKEN

African Chicken Pie

THE DELICATE PUFF PASTRY used as the topping on this pie shows the influence of the Dutch on this recipe. This type of pastry was used daily in the average Dutch household. This recipe was used in South Africa and serves six (6).

- 5-lb. Stewing or Roasting Hen
- 1 large Onion (peeled, quartered)
- 6 whole Allspice
- 4 whole Cloves
- ¼ tsp. Mace
- 1 tsp. Salt
- 6 Peppercorns
- ½ lb. Ham (cubed)
- 3 cups Water
- ½ cup White Wine
- ¼ cup Cream of Wheat
- 2 Egg Yolks
- 2 tbls. Lemon Juice
- 2 Hard-boiled Eggs (sliced)
- 1 Recipe Puff Pastry (see below)
- 1 Egg—beat with 1 tbls. Water and use as coating for pastry.

In a large pot or dutch oven, place chicken, onion, allspice, cloves, mace, salt and peppercorns. Add 3 cups of water and bring all to a boil. Lower the heat, cover and simmer until tender—one to two hours. Then place chicken on a platter to cool. Strain out spices and save 3 cups chicken stock. When chicken is cool, debone chicken and cut into 1-inch pieces and throw the skin away. Next, make sauce as follows: Add wine to chicken stock, bring to a boil and slowly add cream of wheat. Reduce heat to low, stir constantly until thickens. In a small bowl, mix together egg yolks and lemon juice. Stir 3 to 4 tbls. of sauce into yolks and then add yolk mixture to sauce. Bring to a boil for one minute. Then remove from heat.

Place ½ deboned chicken in a baking dish, scatter chopped ham on top, then place a row of egg slices. Redo above and then pour sauce over the two layers.

Make top puff pastry as follows: Cut ¼ lb. sweet butter into two cups of flour until it is the consistency of pie dough. Add 4 to 6 tbls. water and knead into a ball. Flour a board and roll out with a floured rolling pin as you would pie dough. Place on top of baking dish and pinch edges. Brush top with water and egg mixture. Bake at 400 degrees for 15 minutes, reduce heat to 350 degrees and bake for 45 minutes.

MAIN DISHES/CHICKEN

African Chicken and Greens

SOUL FOOD IN AFRICA. This recipe is used widely in Africa especially in the vegetable growing areas. A tasty nutritional dinner that serves four (4).

1 3- to 4-lb. Chicken (cut in pieces)
1 large Onion (chopped)
1 large Carrot (sliced and peeled)
Salt to taste
1 clove Garlic (minced)
1 tsp. ground Coriander
3 tbls. Butter
3 pkgs. (10-oz.) of frozen Spinach or Collard Greens

Put chicken pieces in a large pot with onion, carrots and enough water to cover. Simmer 1 hour until tender. Remove chicken and cool. Save onion and carrots. Discard stock. Melt butter in a large fry pan. Add salt, garlic and coriander. Brown chicken on all sides and remove from pan. Place all (thawed) greens in fry pan—cover with layers of browned chicken. Cover and simmer for 15 to 25 minutes (depending on greens used) and serve with steaming bowl of rice.

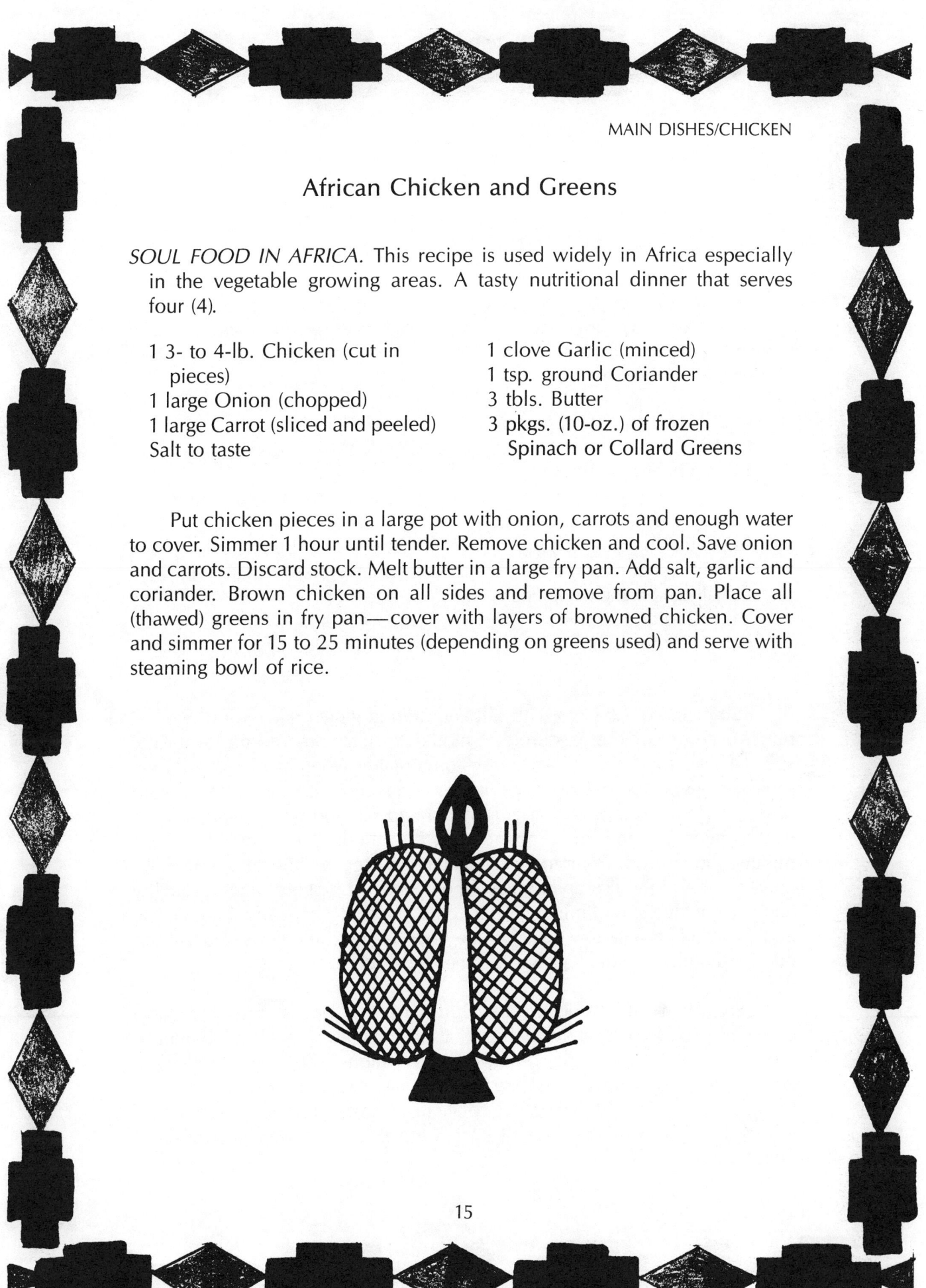

MAIN DISHES/CHICKEN & SHRIMP

Chicken-Goober Stew

PORTUGAL AND AFRICA were both known for the combining of fish and meat dishes. It was historically common in both countries, and it is not known to this day who originally gave whom the idea to cook in this manner. As far as I am concerned, this is *the* most beautiful and healthful dinner one can serve at a dinner party. This recipe originated in West Africa and serves six (6).

- 6 lbs. Chicken (cut in pieces)
- 1 tbls. Salt
- 1 tbls. Ginger (ground)
- ½ cup Peanut Oil
- 1 cup Onion (chop finely)
- 5 medium Tomatoes (chopped)
- 1 small can Tomato Paste
- 1 small can Shrimp (chop finely)
- 1 tsp. Garlic (minced)
- ¼ tsp. Ginger Root
- ½ tsp. Red Pepper
- ½ tsp. White Pepper
- 6 cups Hot Water
- ¼ cup leftover Fish (crumbled)
- 2 whole Chilies
- 1 cup Peanut Butter and 1 cup Cold Water to make into a paste
- 12 large Okra (wash and stem)
- 6 Hard-boiled Eggs

Rub pieces of Chicken with salt and ground ginger. Heat oil in 6 quart dutch oven or cooking casserole at moderate heat. Brown chicken on all sides, 4 pieces at a time. Place pieces on a platter when browned and then saute onions at low heat for 5 minutes. Add chopped tomatoes, tomato paste, chopped shrimp, garlic, ginger root and red and white pepper. Raise heat to high. Stir and bring mixture to a boil. Reduce heat and simmer 3 minutes uncovered. Pour in 6 cups of hot water, a little at a time. Stir constantly. Add the fish and chilies. Then add the chicken. Mix thoroughly and cook at low heat 15 minutes uncovered. Next, stir in peanut butter paste and okra and cook at low heat for one hour. Cover during this hour—then add hard-boiled whole eggs and simmer for 5 more minutes.

Serve with fufu (African Yam Dumplings) or rice and garnish with chopped fresh fruits and vegetables that are in season, such as: bananas, pineapple, cantelope, papaya, strawberries, onions, broccoli, cauliflower, etc. and roasted peanuts. Serve each fruit or vegetable in its own individual bowl. (Place the rice or fufu on your plate first, cover with stew and build on top of the stew with any and all fresh vegetables and fruits you wish. A fantastic taste!

MAIN DISHES/BEEF/LAMB

Africans use much more lamb than beef; however, this whole section can be interchanged with either Lamb or Beef—your tastebuds and your pocketbook will dictate what you use.

Dried Fruit Curry

THIS RECIPE originated in South Africa and serves four (4). It should be noted that any recipe using raisins, dates, and rice were greatly influenced by the Arabs of the East who brought many of the spices of the East into the art of African cooking.

    1 cup Dried Apples   2 tbls. Curry
    ½ cup Prunes or Dates (chop)   2 tbls. Red Wine Vinegar
    ½ cup Raisins   1 tbls. Lemon Juice
    1½ cup Water
    1½ to 2 lbs. boneless Beef or   Garnish:
        Lamb (cubed)   1 tbls. Salted Peanuts
    1 tsp. Salt   (chopped)
    2 tbls. Vegetable Oil   2 medium Bananas (sliced)
    1 cup Onion (chopped)

Place apples, prunes or dates in a pot and pour in 1½ cups water. Cook at a low heat for 1 hour. Stir 2 to 3 times during this hour. In a large skillet, heat the oil at moderate heat. Brown the meat in 2 or 3 batches and place on a platter when browned and set aside. Pour off from skillet all but 2 tbls. of fat and drop in onions and saute for 3 minutes at moderate heat. Then, lower heat and add curry. Next return the meat with liquid, apples, prunes, raisins and their juice. Add lemon juice and vinegar and bring to a boil. Then reduce heat and simmer uncovered for 1 hour. Add water if needed, but when tender, most of the moisture will be gone. Place on a platter, sprinkle with peanuts and arrange sliced bananas around it. Serve with a steaming bowl of rice.

MAIN DISHES/BEEF/LAMB

Sosaties

THIS IS a South African recipe and serves four (4). It is a marinated, grilled meat. Sosaties seemed to have originated in Malaysia from Malay Sate which means "spiced sauce" and Sesate which means "meat on a skewer." Sosatie is to an African what Shish-Kebab is to an Afgani. The ancient street hawkers of Africa would carry bamboo yokes on their shoulders. Hanging from this yoke would be a charcoal brazier on one end and a series of little dishes in a wicker basket on the other end. At the hint of a cent, the hawker would sit down, take out sosaties already marinated and skewered and grill them in front of you on the brazier.

  2 lbs. Lamb Chops or
  2 lbs. Sirloin Tip Steaks
  10 dried Apricots
  3 tbls. Oil
  3 large Onions (sliced)
  1 clove Garlic (chopped)

  6 fresh Grape Leaves
      (chop)—optional
  3 tbls. Wine Vinegar
  12 slices of Bacon
  2 tbls. Sour Cream
  Pinch Cayenne Pepper

Soak apricots in water for two hours. Simmer until tender and press through a sieve or colander, or puree in a blender. Place oil in a skillet and brown garlic and onion slices. Add apricot pulp, cayenne, grape leaves, salt and vinegar. Cook at moderate heat for 3 minutes. Take off burner and cool.

In a bowl, make layers of lamb or beef, bacon slices and apricot marinade. Marinate overnight. Take meat out the next day, cut in large cubes, wrap with bacon and skewer. Charcoal over coals.

Add water to marinade in a sauce pan to thin out slightly. Then add sour cream and bring to a boil and turn off. This becomes the sauce for the meat. This too is excellent with a bowl of steaming rice.

MAIN DISHES/BEEF/LAMB

Bootjiebredie

BEAN STEW FROM CAPETOWN, South Africa is a recipe that serves four (4). Bredies are basically the African form of goulash. It is very similar to the mixed meat and vegetable dishes that were popular in Europe for years. Bredies differ because of the delicacy of the spices!

- 2 lbs. Lamb Chops or
- 2 lbs. Beef Stew
- Salt and Pepper to taste
- Flour as needed
- 3 Onions (diced)
- 2 tbls. Fat or Suet
- 1 lb. Green Beans
- 2 tbls. Savory Spices
- 6 potatoes (peeled and sliced)
- 4 Tomatoes (chopped)
- 2 Green Peppers (chopped)
- 4 flowerets Cauliflower
- 1 cup Peas (fresh or frozen)
- 1 bunch Parsley (chopped)
- ½ Pear

Cut lamb or beef into cubes and salt and pepper the cubes. Then roll them in flour. Heat fat in skillet and brown the meat on all sides. Dice 3 onions and also brown the onions with the meat. Clean green beans (cut off tips) and add beans to skillet. Next add sliced potatoes and ½ cup water. Place all items in fry pan into a large pot or dutch oven. Simmer 1 hour at lower heat (covered). Add a little water if needed.

Cook pear in a small saucepan in some sugar and water until soft, add to meat mixture along with tomatoes, green pepper, cauliflower, savory spices and peas. Cook 10 more minutes. If gravy needs thickening, mix 1 to 3 tbls. cornstarch in ¼ cup of water and add to pot. Bring to a boil and thicken. Serve with hot rolls or injera and garnish with chopped parsley.

MAIN DISHES/BEEF/LAMB

Bobotie

CURRIED LAMB OR BEEF WITH CUSTARD TOPPING is a recipe which originated in South Africa and serves four (4). Bobotie is to South Africa what Moussaka is to Greece. Every South African household may have their own little special variation of this dish. The background of Bobotie goes back to 1609 when a poet named Leipoldt, who had eaten a dish similar to Bobotie in Europe at the time, traced its beginnings to Malaysia. He noted that as of 1652, "Johns Company's Kitchen Garden's," a famous restaurant opened at the Cape of Good Hope, served Bobotie as its specialty. The meat was always ground or minced since the cattle used was tough, and also, many times, wild game was used in the original recipes.

1 slice White Bread (break into 1-inch pieces)	1 medium tart Apple (peel, grate)
1 cup Milk	½ cup Raisins
2 tbls. Butter	¼ cup Almonds (chopped)
2 lbs. Ground Lamb or	1 tbls. Brown Sugar
2 lbs. Ground Chuck	½ tsp. Black Pepper
1½ cups Onions (chopped)	3 Eggs
2 tbls. Curry	4 Orange or Lemon Leaves or substitute Bay Leaves
1 tsp. Salt	
¼ cup Lemon Juice	

Preheat oven to 300 degrees. Mix bread in milk in a bowl and let stand for 10 minutes. In a large skillet, melt butter, add lamb or beef and cook over moderate heat. Stir often, mash lumps. Cook until well done and in granules. Pour off fat. Save 2 tbls. of fat. Next add onions to meat and cook for 5 minutes. Add curry, sugar, salt and pepper and cook for 2 minutes. Stir in lemon juice and bring to a boil. Take off the heat.

Drain bread through a sieve, squeeze dry and save the milk. Place bread in a small bowl, add 1 egg, apple, raisins and almonds. Mix and then add all to meat mixture. Mix thoroughly. Pack this lamb or beef mixture into a 3-quart souffle or baking dish. Smooth flat. Tuck in orange, lemon or bay leaves. With a mixer, beat remaining 2 eggs with the leftover milk until frothy. Pour over the meat mixture. Bake in 300-degree oven for 30 minutes until golden brown.

Note: The cooking of Bobotie is important. DO NOT make the oven too

MAIN DISHES/BEEF/LAMB

hot. DO NOT cook too long. It should be moist and eaten with a steaming bowl of rice. If orange or lemon leaves are available and used instead of bay leaves, the flavor of the Bobotie will be much more delicate!

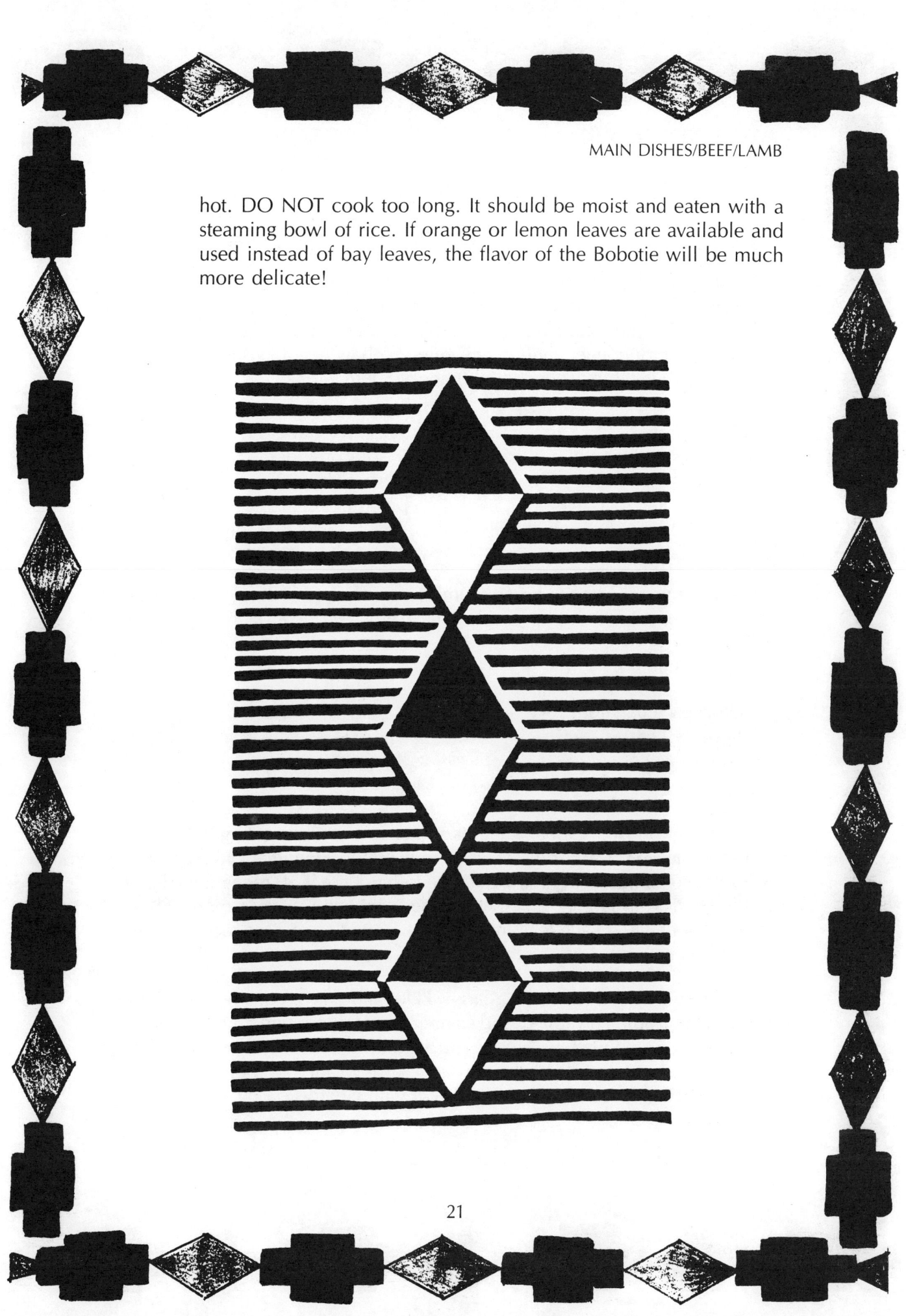

MAIN DISHES/BEEF/LAMB

Frikkadels

STUFFED CABBAGE ROLLS, South African style. This recipe serves four to six. Frikkadels can be served stuffed in the cabbage roll or just as a patty by itself. It is interesting to serve a combination thereof and place them on a platter surrounding a mound of Geelrys (yellow rice and raisins) pg. 46. This recipe is the seasoned hamburger of South Africa.

FILLING:
2 lbs. Ground Lamb or
2 lbs. Ground Chuck
½ cup Bread Crumbs
½ cup Onion (chop finely)
2 eggs
¼ tsp. Nutmeg
1 tsp. Coriander
2 tsp. Salt
pinch of Pepper
¼ cup Vegetable Oil

Mix lamb or beef with bread crumbs, onions, eggs, nutmeg, coriander, salt and pepper in a bowl. Knead until mixed thoroughly. Divide into 12 balls
2 inches round.

Cabbage Preparation:
1 large head Cabbage
2 cups Beef Stock (canned)
2 tbls. Flour
½ cup Water
Salt and Pepper to taste

Trim off bruised cabbage leaves. Place cabbage in a large pot with enough water to cover. Bring to a boil and boil ten minutes. Take out and cool. Take off tender leaves. If you come to harder leaves, repeat the above process until you have 12 unbroken tender cabbage leaves or more. Place one ball of filling in each leaf and fold leaf around meat. Use toothpicks to fasten, if necessary.

Place the 12 Frikkadels in a large skillet and add 2 cups of beef stock and bring to a boil. Lower heat and simmer, covered, for one hour. Take rolls out and place on a platter. Thicken sauce with flour and water made into a smooth paste and add slowly to the sauce. Bring sauce to a boil and pour thickened sauce over cabbage rolls. Serve with Geelrys on pg. 46.

MAIN DISHES/LAMB

Mock Venison

MANY MUTTON AND LAMB dishes are marinated in Africa not only for the tantalizing flavor, but also for the tenderizing effect since so much of the livestock has been run for so long in Africa. Mock Venison is not only a tasty dish but also a dish of beauty. It is important that the meat marinate for 24 hours—too long and the meat may lose its texture and become too sour. Be sure to turn it every few hours. This recipe originated in South Africa and serves six (6).

6 lbs. Leg of Lamb

Marinade:
  1 cup Red Wine Vinegar
  2 tbls. Sugar
  ¼ tsp. ground Ginger
  6 whole Cloves
  1 large Onion (sliced thin)

End of Marinade . . .

2 cloves Garlic (minced)
3 tsp. Salt
1 tsp. Pepper
2 tbls. Vegetable Oil
2 cups Hot Water
2 tbls. Apricot Jam
½ cup Raisins
¼ lb. Bacon (cut in ¾' strips)
1 tbls. Flour
2 tbls. Cold Water

In a large pan or bowl, marinate for 24 hours (turning every few hours) the leg of lamb in vinegar, sugar, ginger, cloves and onion slices.

Take lamb out of marinade and cut 1" slits on all sides of the leg. In each slit: place 1 strip bacon, 3 raisins and a piece of garlic. Rub the salt and pepper all over the leg. Place it in a covered roasting pan that has 2 tbls. oil in it. Heat on stove—browning leg of lamb on all sides until golden brown. Remove from heat and pour marinade over leg. Cover roaster and bake for 1 hour and 15 minutes at 400 degrees for rare and up to 2 hours if you prefer well done. Place on platter and cover it with foil.

Sauce: Skim fat off from marinade in roaster. Add apricot jam and make a paste out of flour and water. Stir into marinade. Bring to a boil and thicken. Place some over lamb and serve rest of sauce in a separate bowl. Delicious served with red cabbage and one of the Yam Dishes as well as the African's steaming bowl of rice.

MAIN DISHES/LAMB

Afrikander (Boer Lamb Chops)

TO KNOW the meaning of "Boer" is the hint as to where this recipe originated. "Boer" (Boor) was the Dutch word for "farmer." To be a Boer in early South Africa meant "one was an aristocrat in the colonial society of the South African Cape." This is a South African recipe and serves four (4).

1 cup Tomato Sauce
3 tbls. Vinegar
1 tbls. Worcestershire
2 grated Onions
1 tbls. Dry Mustard
1 Beef Bouillon Cube
Salt and Pepper to taste

8 Lamb Chops
2 tbls. Butter
½ cup Cream
2 tbls. Celery (chopped)
2 tbls. Carrot (chopped)
2 tbls. Leek (chopped)

Place tomato sauce in a bowl and mix in the vinegar, Worcestershire, onions, mustard, salt and pepper. Marinate lamb chops for 1 hour in sauce and take out and dry chops. Fry in a skillet in butter until browned. Keep meat pink on inside. Bring marinade to a boil in a separate saucepan. Add cream, beef bouillon, celery, carrots and leek. Cook at moderate heat for 10 minutes. Serve sauce over rare lamb chop. Red wine is delicious with this dish. And, of course, this dish can be served with a steaming bowl of rice.

ANOTHER WAY from South Africa.

South African Lamb Chops

12 Lamb Chops
1 8-oz. can Tomato Sauce
¼ cup Vinegar
1 Onion minced

2 tbls. Worcestershire
1 tsp. Dry Mustard
1 tsp. Salt

Mix tomato sauce, vinegar, onion, Worcestershire, mustard and salt in a large bowl. Marinate chops for one hour. Remove chops and dry them with paper towels. Pan fry chops until brown and tender and serve with heated marinade sauce.

MAIN DISHES/COMBO MEATS

Segana Dora Wat (Sā gäh näh Dōrō Wäht)

THIS LAMB AND CHICKEN recipe which originated in Ethiopia and serves six (6). Again, another variation of the "National Dish" of Ethiopia, namely the WATS! . . .

4 cups Onion (sliced)
8 tbls. Butter
2 lbs. Stewing Lamb (cubed)
½ cup Lemon Juice
1 3-lb. Chicken (cut in pieces)
4 tbls. Flour (dissolved in water to form a paste)
½ tsp. Berbere' (or Red Pepper)
½ tsp. Paprika
½ tsp. Ginger
Salt and Pepper to taste
8 Carrots (peeled and cut in 2-inch rounds)
2 Tomatoes (sliced)
8 Hard-boiled Eggs (peeled)

In a large pot or dutch oven, brown onion slices in 8 tbls. butter. Add lamb, lemon juice and enough water to cover. Braise at moderate heat for 30 minutes, covered. Add chicken. Braise 30 minutes more. Then add all spices, carrots and tomatoes along with flour paste mix and reduce heat to low. Simmer 30 minutes more. Poke eggs with fork and add to stew. Simmer 3 more minutes and serve over hot rice, noodles or kil kil. Always serve the Wats with Injera.

MAIN DISHES/COMBO MEATS

Meat Lagos

LAGOS IS the Capital City of Nigeria, thus it is easy to see where this recipe originated! This recipe originated in Nigeria and serves four (4).

- ½ lb. Beef (cubed)
- ½ lb. Pork (cubed)
- ½ lb. Lamb (cubed)
- 1 cup Water
- ½ cup Spinach or Collards
- 1 large Onion (chopped)
- ½ cup sliced Tomatoes
- ½ cup Green Pepper (cut in strips)
- ½ cup Vegetable Oil
- Salt and Pepper to taste

Place meat in a large pot and add water and onions. Cover and simmer for 30 to 40 minutes until all meat is tender. Then add the tomatoes, green pepper, oil and simmer ten more minutes. Add the greens and simmer 20 minutes more. Serve hot. Meat Lagos is good with rice, potatoes, cornbread or fufu balls.

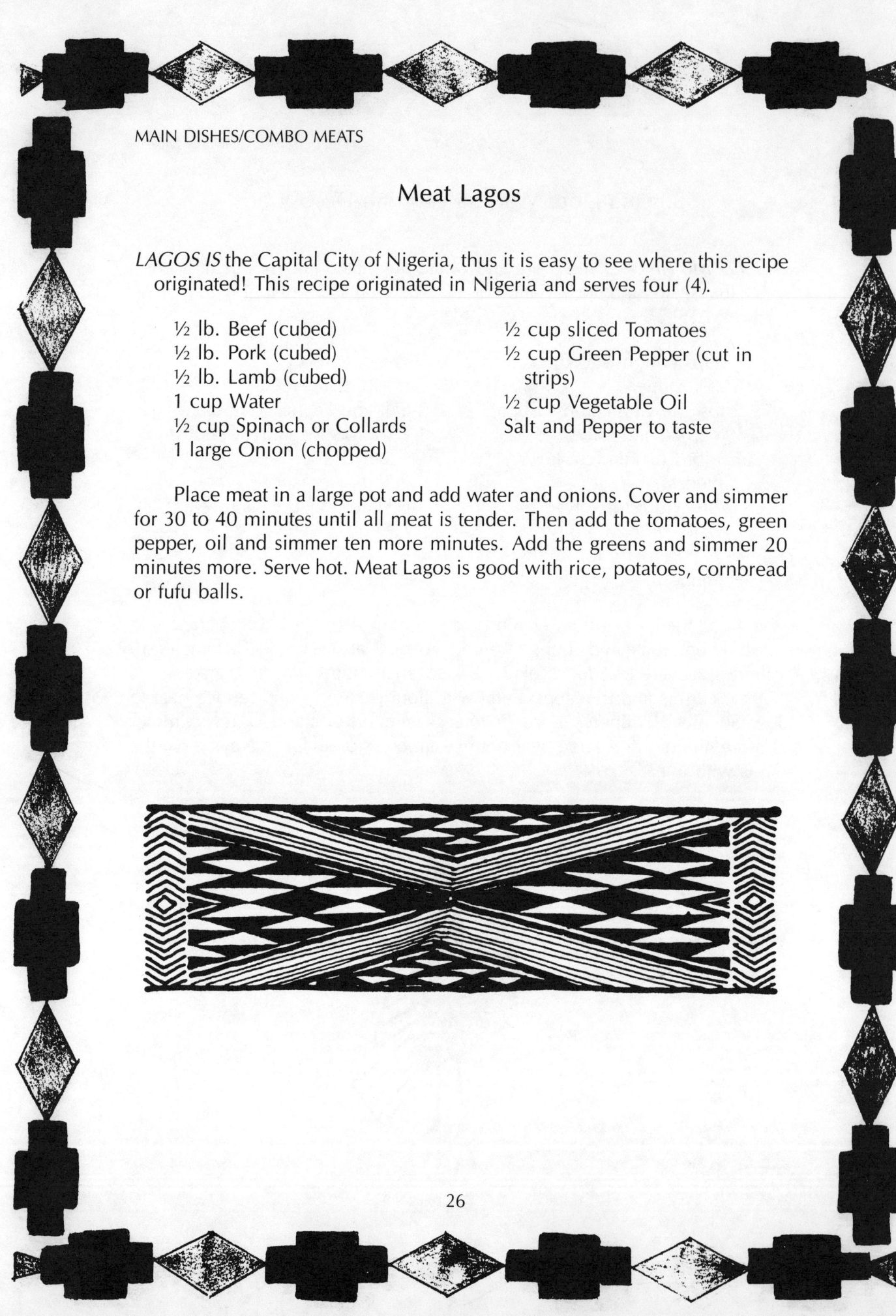

MAIN DISHES/DUCK

Zanzibar Duck (Zähn zē bär)

ZANZIBAR WAS well-known for the trading of slaves and spices. Cloves is the most important spice and scent of Zanzibar. Rice is served with most Zanzibari meals since an ancient Persian custom is to serve rice as it was always done at the banquets of the Sultans. This recipe originated in East Africa and serves four (4).

1 5-lb. Duck
¼ cup Vegetable Oil
2 cups Chicken Broth
12 whole Cloves
1 Hot Chili Pepper (stem and seed)
½ cup Orange Juice
2 tbls. Lime Juice
½ cup Red Bell Pepper (chopped)
¼ tsp. Salt
Orange wedges studded with Cloves for garnish

Preheat oven to 350 degrees. Pat duck dry and remove fat from cavity. Poke duck around thighs, lower breast and back with a sharp knife. In a large dutch oven or roaster, heat oil over moderate heat. Add duck and brown in oil on all sides for about 15 minutes. Place duck on a platter and discard fat. Add 1 cup chicken broth to roaster and bring to a boil. Stir in cloves, chili pepper and turn off heat. Place duck in liquid, place in oven, cover and bake for 1 hour at 350 degrees. Take out of oven, place duck on a platter. Skim off as much fat as possible and discard. Also discard chili pepper and cloves. Then add 1 cup chicken broth to what is left and stir and scrape brown bits into liquid. Bring to a boil. Next add orange juice, lime juice, bell pepper and salt. Return duck to pan and baste with sauce. Cover and bake 20 more minutes. Baste again. Serve with sauce and a steaming bowl of rice. A very pleasant accompaniment to this recipe is the steamed Papaya found on page 51.

MAIN DISHES/FROM THE SEA

Gesmoorde Vis (Cod and Potatoes in Tomato Sauce)

THE WORD "SMOOR" found in Gesmoorde means braising or smothering. This fish is first smothered in water to remove the salt and then braised with onion, chilies, etc. until golden brown. This recipe originated in South Africa and serves four (4).

1 lb. Salt Cod	3 small Onions (sliced)
3 medium Potatoes	1 tbls. Hot Chilies
4 medium Tomatoes	1 tsp. Garlic (minced)
3 tbls. Vegetable Oil	1 tbls. Brown Sugar
1 bunch Parsley	1 Lemon (cut in 6 wedges)

To prepare recipe: Place cod in cold water for 12 hours before cooking (smothered in water). Drain and rinse cod by changing water 3 times during the soaking. Then drain cod and cut into 1-inch cubes. Boil the tomatoes for one minute and rinse with cold water. Peel and cut into slices.

Next, in a large skillet heat oil and cook onions for 10 minutes at moderate heat until browned. Add tomatoes, chilies, garlic, sugar and cook until liquid is almost evaporated. Stir in cod and potatoes. Cover and simmer at low heat for 25 minutes. Garnish with lemon and parsley.

Ingelegde Vis

ORIGINALLY THIS RECIPE had a Malay background. Each Malay household and each Afrikeenar household had its own ideas on how to prepare this recipe. Since there was no refrigeration years ago, it was important to learn ways to preserve fish to be used by the people and especially the sailors at sea. This method became as important as salting for preservation. The pickled fish were put either in screw top bottles (which were not too plentiful) or in the tin cans that were emptied from a popular golden syrup to be used when needed. If the fish was in the tin cans, the local carpenter would solder the top on to make them air tight. This recipe serves six (6).

¾ cup Vegetable Oil
2 lbs. Halibut Steaks
3 Onions (sliced)
½ cup Brown Sugar
3 tbls. Hot Chilies
2 cups Vinegar

3 tbls. Curry
1 tbls. Ginger Root
2 Bay Leaves
1 tsp. Coriander
2 tsp. Salt
1 cup Water

48 hours ahead of time—heat ½ cup of oil in a large skillet at moderate heat. Place fish in oil and fry 3 minutes on each side until golden brown. Drain on a paper towel. Discard oil in skillet and add ¼ cup fresh oil. Saute Onions until golden brown over moderate heat. Add sugar, chilies, curry, ginger, bay leaves (crumpled), and coriander and salt. Cook over low heat for 2 minutes. Add vinegar and water, raise heat and bring to a boil. Then lower heat and simmer for 10 minutes.

Remove skin and bone from halibut and cut fish into cubes. Place ⅓ of the fish into a bowl and cover with 1 cup marinade above. Do the same process twice more. Place 2 bay leaves crumpled on top and cover bowl with plastic wrap. Place in refrigerator for two days before serving. Serve hot or cold.

MAIN DISHES/FROM THE SEA

Wali Na Samaki (Wäh lē Näh Säh mäh kē)

A FISH AND RICE recipe that originated in Tanzania, East Africa and serves eight (8). Many recipes in Tanzania such as this one were widely influenced by German missionaries many years ago.

- 4 large Tomatoes (sliced)
- 2 Green Peppers (sliced)
- 2 Onions (chopped)
- 2 cups Water
- Juice and Peel of 1 Lemon
- 1 tbls. Salt
- 1 tbls. Pepper
- ½ cup Vegetable Oil
- 2 Bay Leaves
- 4 lbs. Red Snapper or Halibut
- 1 cup Flour
- 4 cups Raw Rice (Cook Rice as per directions on package)

Cook the following in a large saucepan over moderate heat for 25 minutes: tomatoes, green pepper, onions, lemon juice, lemon peel, salt, pepper, water, oil, and bay leaves.

Cut fish into 4-oz. pieces and rub with salt and pepper. Dip in flour. Brown in ½" hot oil until brown and tender. Serve as follows: Place cooked rice on a large platter. Place fish on top of rice and pour sauce over everything.

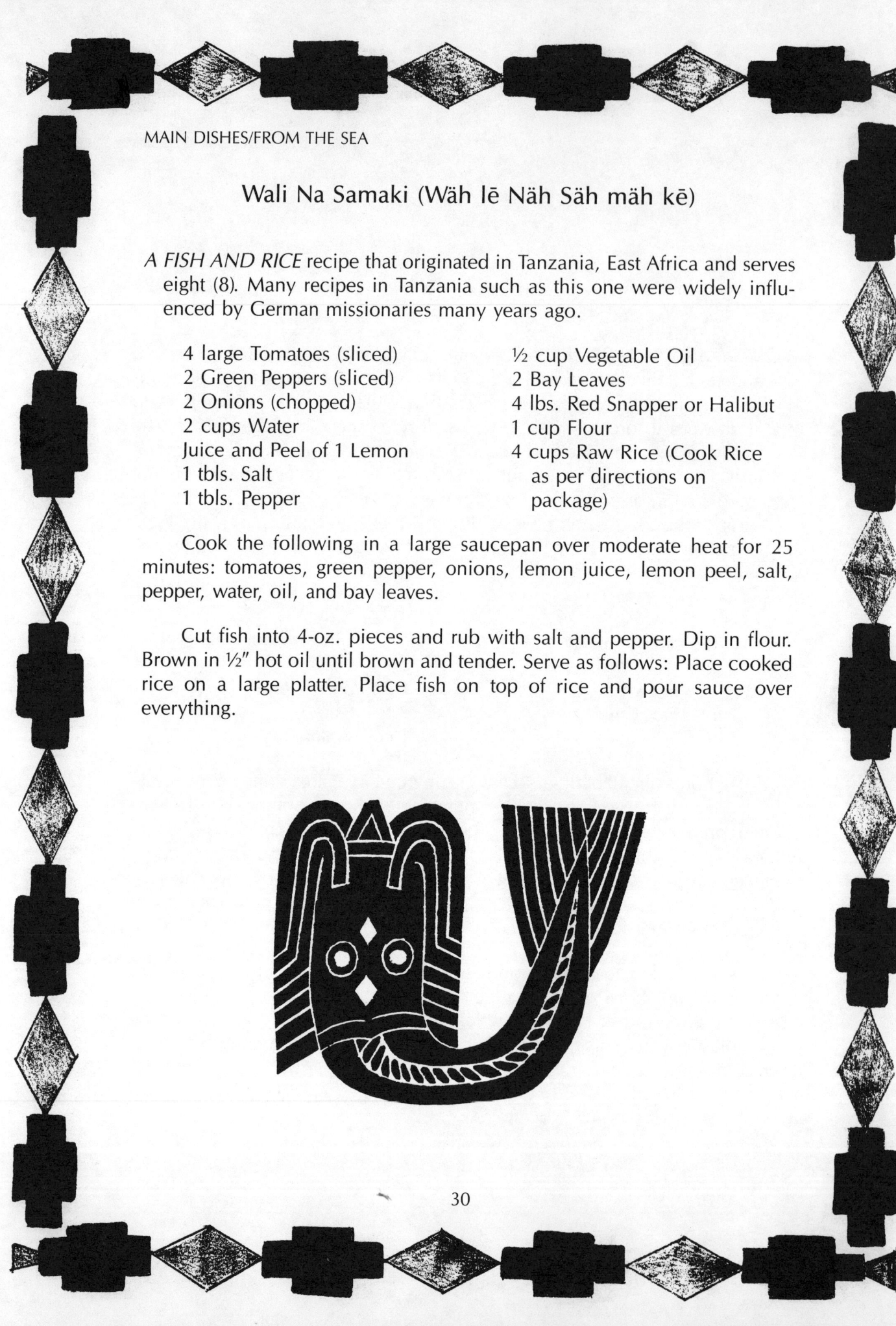

MAIN DISHES/FROM THE SEA

Yoruba (Yō rōō bǎ)

FISH STEW that originated in Nigeria and serves four (4). A Yoruba Proverb says "The man that eats no pepper is weak, pepper is the staff of life. . . "

2 lbs. Fish Fillets (cut into thin slices)
   (Can use Red Snapper, Bluefish or Striped Bass)

Salt to taste
Pinch of Thyme on each fillet
¼ cup Red Bell Pepper
   (crushed)
6 oz. Tomato Paste

1 medium Onion (chopped)
4 cups Water
¼ cup Peanut Oil
1 Chicken Bouillon Cube

Season fish with salt and thyme and set aside. In a large pot, place the crushed red peppers, tomato paste, onion and water. Cook 10 minutes over moderate heat. Add oil and bouillon cube. Simmer at low heat for 15 more minutes. Then add the fish slices and simmer 10 minutes. A steaming bowl of rice goes well with this dish.

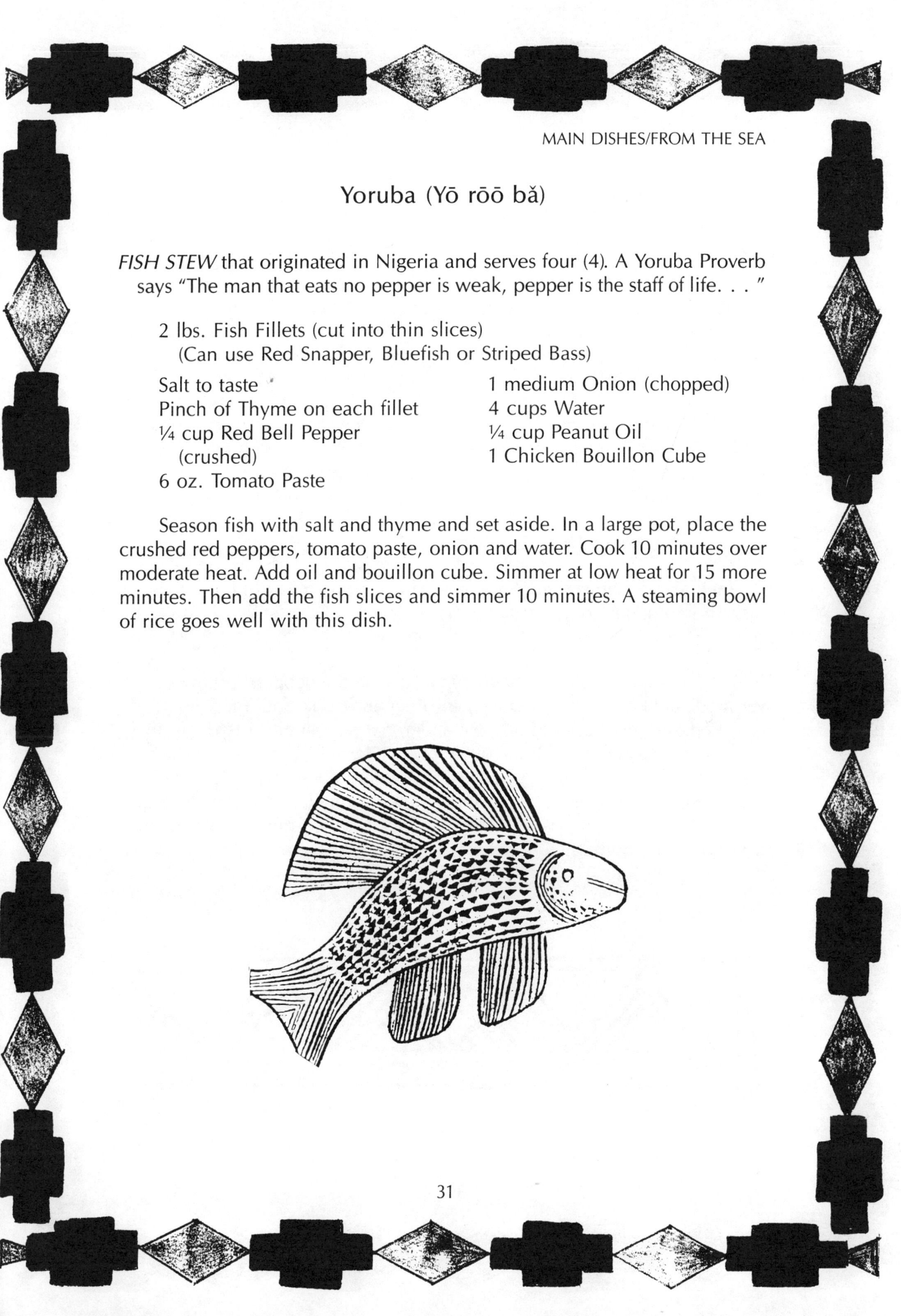

MAIN DISHES/FROM THE SEA

Peixe a Lumbo (Pā ēx ā äh Lūmbō)

SHRIMP AND FISH STEW that originated in Mozambique, South Africa and serves four (4). There is known Portuguese influence upon many of the recipes of Mozambique. This nation being a coastal area, fishing becomes a very important food source. Also, Mozambique is well-known for its Coconut Farms and the coconut milk in this recipe adds a magic richness to this seafood delight.

1 lb. medium Shrimp (raw)	2 Green Peppers (chop finely)
8 4-oz. Sea Bass or Snapper Pieces	2 Tomatoes (chop finely)
	1 tbls. Coriander
1½ tsp. Salt	1 tsp. Hot Red Pepper
3 tbls. Olive Oil	½ cup Coconut Milk
1½ cups Onion (chop finely)	

Shell and devein shrimp. Slice down back with knife and lift out vein. Wash shrimp under cold water and drain. Sprinkle fish steaks with salt on each side.

In a large skillet, heat oil. Saute onions and green peppers for 5 minutes over moderate heat. Add tomatoes, stir often and cook until most liquid is gone. Remove from heat and add coriander, red pepper and 1 tsp. salt. In a large cooking casserole or Dutch oven, place a layer of ½ of the fish, next a layer of shrimp, then a layer of coated vegetables above and repeat layers again. Last, pour in coconut milk and simmer 5 minutes at moderate heat. Reduce heat to low and partly cover. Simmer 12 to 15 minutes. Delicious served with rice or mashed potatoes.

MAIN DISHES/FROM THE SEA

Couscous (Kōōs Kōōs)

A SHRIMP DISH originating in North Africa and serves six (6).

1 Hot Chili (minced)
4 Tomatoes (chopped)
2 Green Peppers (seeded, diced)
1½ cups Olive Oil or Vegetable Oil
1 Onion (chopped)
1 clove Garlic (minced)
Salt and Pepper to taste
2 lbs. Shrimp (shell and devein)

1 can Hearts of Palm (sliced)
1¼ cups Chicken Broth
1 pkg. frozen Peas
1 cup Black Olives (chopped)
2 cups Yellow Corn Meal
½ cup Farina
3 Scallions (minced)
3 tbls. Parsley (chopped)
2 Hard-boiled Eggs (chopped)

Garnish with: 1 head of Lettuce
4 Hard-boiled eggs
½ cup seeded Black Olives
2 Tomatoes (cut in wedges)

Place ½ cup water in a blender along with hot chili, tomatoes, green peppers. Puree all (may take more than one batch to finish). Heat ¾ cup oil in large skillet—sauté onions and garlic for 2 minutes over moderate heat. Add tomato-pepper puree and salt and pepper and simmer at low heat for 5 minutes. Chop all shrimp except 6 and add to sauce and simmer 5 more minutes. Then take off heat and set aside. In another large skillet place the other ¾ cup oil. In a bowl, mix corn meal, farina, scallions, parsley and 1 tsp. salt. Add this to heated oil and stir for 1 to 2 minutes. Then add shrimp mixture to it along with chopped eggs and take off heat.

Now oil a 5-quart pot or dutch oven and place over a double boiler with 2 cups water. At bottom of 5 quart pan, place 6 whole shrimp, sliced heart of palm, 1 sliced egg. Pour in Couscous mixture and place over double boiler. Cook at low heat 1½ to 2 hours. If you need more water, add often and keep about 1 inch in pot. When done, invert pan immediately over a large platter. Let it set 10 minutes and then remove pan. Garnish with lettuce, eggs, olives, tomato wedges.

MAIN DISHES/FROM THE SEA

Nigerian Crabs and Rice

THIS RECIPE ORIGINATED in Nigeria which in its southern most part is the coastal area known as the Slave Coast. Fishing and trapping supply a lot of the food to this area. The Niger River and the Benue River empty into the Gulf of Guinea and this low-laying coastal area is perfect for the growing of rice and the trapping of crabs.

- 1 quart Water
- 2 cups Brown Rice
- 2 Bell Peppers (shredded)
- 1 large Onion (sliced)
- 2 tbls. Curry
- 8 large Crabs or 1½ lbs. Crabmeat
- 2 tbls. Peanut Oil
- ½ tsp. Red Pepper Flakes
- ½ lb. Raw Shrimp (peeled)
- 1 tsp. Salt

Cook the 2 cups brown rice in 1 quart of water for 25 minutes. Sauté green pepper, crabmeat, shrimp, onions and red pepper in peanut oil for 2 minutes at moderate heat. Add curry and salt and cook until onion is golden brown. Add cooked rice and stir and simmer 10 more minutes. Serve immediately.

Vegetables

Spicy Okra

THIS RECIPE originated in West Africa and serves four (4).

- 8 cups Water
- ½ cup Onions (chopped finely)
- 1 tsp. Garlic (chopped finely)
- 1 tsp. Red Pepper
- 1 tsp. White Pepper
- 2 tsp. Salt
- 1 lb. large fresh Okra (Wash, remove stem and cut in 3 pieces)

In a large saucepan, mix water, onions, garlic, red and white pepper and salt. Bring to a boil over high heat. Place okra in water and lower heat to medium. Cook 15 minutes. Drain in colander. Rinse with cold water and place in bowl and cover. Serve warm or cold.

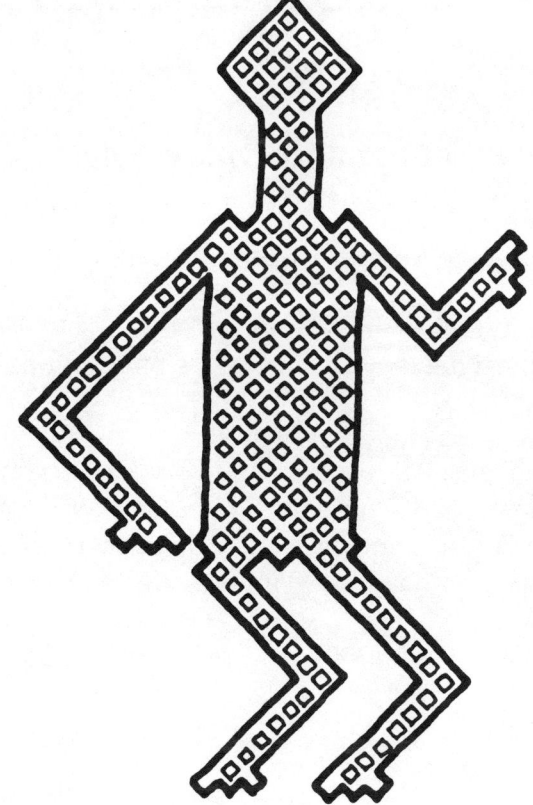

VEGETABLES

Spicy Diced Tomato Salad

THIS RECIPE originated in West Africa and seves four (4).

    4 large Tomatoes   ½ tsp. Red Pepper
    2 tbls. Lemon Juice   1 tsp. Salt

Place tomatoes in boiling water and boil 10 seconds. Place in colander and rinse with cold water. Peel tomatoes and chop finely. In a medium bowl, mix lemon juice, red pepper and salt. Add tomatoes, toss gently and marinate at room temperature for 30 minutes. Serve at room temperature or cold from the refrigerator.

Red Beet and Onion Salad

THIS RECIPE originated in South Africa and serves four (4).

    1 lb. fresh Red Beets   ½ tsp. Sugar
    ¼ cup Red Wine Vinegar   2 small Onions (sliced)
    1 tsp. Salt

Cut tops from beets, wash and place in salted boiling water. Reduce heat, cover and simmer for 30 minutes. Drain and cool. Then peel beets and slice. In a deep bowl, mix vinegar, salt and sugar. Place beets and sliced onions in mixture and marinate for 30 minutes. Turn beets every 10 minutes.

Red Cabbage can be chopped and prepared in the same manner as above.

VEGETABLES

Cucumber-Chili Salad

THIS RECIPE originated in South Africa and serves four (4). An excellent compliment to Frikkadels.

- 2 large Cucumbers (peel and cut into ⅛ inch rounds)
- 1½ tsp. Salt
- 3 tbls. Red Wine Vinegar
- ½ tsp. Sugar
- 2 tsp. Hot Chilies (chopped finely)

Mix salt, vinegar and sugar in a bowl, add cucumbers and chilies. Toss gently and serve at once.

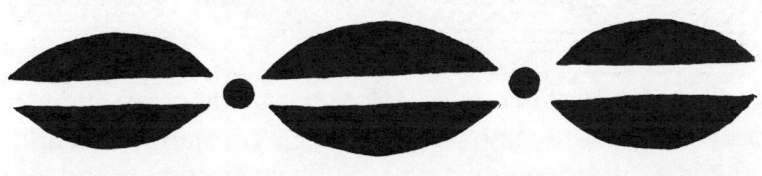

Avocado-Ginger Salad

THIS RECIPE originated in West Africa and serves four (4).

- 2 large Avocados
- 2 tbls. Lemon Juice
- 1 tsp. ground Ginger
- 1 tsp. Salt

Cut avocados in half. Remove seed, brown skin and outer shell. Cut into ½-inch cubes. In a bowl, combine lemon juice, ginger and salt. Add avocado cubes, toss gently and marinate at room temperature for 30 minutes. Serve at room temperature or after refrigerated for one to two hours.

VEGETABLES

Green Bean Atjar

THIS RECIPE originated in Java and was brought to Capetown, South Africa by the Javanese. It became extremely popular. It is known as a Chutney dish and served in place of what we know as the Western Salad. Every Javanese District had its own type of Atjar. The word Atjar means "a variety of pickles." This recipe serves six (6).

- 2 lbs. fresh Green Beans (trim, wash and quarter)
- 2 tbls. Salt
- 1½ cups Oil
- 2 tbls. Curry
- 2 tsp. Turmeric
- 2 tbls. Hot Chilies (chopped)
- 1 tsp. Fenugreek Seeds (crush)
- 1 tsp. Garlic (minced)

Place beans in a deep bowl and pour in enough boiling water to cover. Let stand 3 minutes. Drain through a colander and run cold water over them. Place beans back in bowl, add salt and cover with plastic wrap and let stand 2 hours at room temperature. Drain beans again and place in 1-quart sterilized jar or a crock.

In a small skillet, heat ¼ cup oil at low heat. Add curry and turmeric and stir. Then add chilies, garlic and fenugreek. Stir constantly and add other oil. Cook 5 minutes. Pour hot oil mix over the beans in the jar and let cool for 1 hour. Cover and refrigerate two days before serving.

VEGETABLES

Yams

YAMS ARE the native food of Africa and one of the most important staples of the country. Yam dishes are used to celebrate everything from marriages, to births, to deaths.

Yams may be prepared in a number of different ways. Here are a few simple suggestions taken from recipes used on Yam Celebration days.

1) Parboil several yams, cool and peel. Slice into rounds and brown in palm-nut oil (which is peanut oil in this country).
2) Parboil, cool and peel several yams. Slice and layer them into a buttered baking dish with layers of finely sliced onions, grated cheese of your choice and bread crumbs. Bake for 15 minutes at 350 degrees.
3) Bake whole yams at 350 degrees for 45 minutes, slice open and serve hot with dark brown sugar and cinnamon.

VEGETABLES

FuFu Dumplings (Yam Paste Balls)

THIS RECIPE originated in West Africa and serves six (6). It is served as a dinner accompaniment as well as commonly served on the many Yam Feast Days that are still popular throughout Africa.

1½ lbs. of Yams   2 cups Water
2 tsp. Salt

Peel and dice yams. Boil in 2 cups water and 2 tsp. salt until very tender. Drain in a colander. Puree yams by mashing into a very fine paste.

To shape FuFu Balls, fill a bowl with cold water and set a plate beside it. Place a little water on the plate, moisten hands and place ¼ cup yam paste in hands rolling it into a firm ball. Place on plate. Moisten hands and repeat process. Makes about 10 balls. Serve balls on platter or place in stews just before serving.

VEGETABLES

Yam or Sweet Potato Stew

PEASANTS IN Africa live on milk, curds and whey, vegetables and cereals. Tubers such as Yams and Sweet Potatoes are a very important part of their diet. This recipe originated in South Africa and serves six (6).

2 lbs. Sweet Potatoes or Yams
¼ cup Brown Sugar
1 tbls. Flour
1 tsp. Salt

4 tbls. Butter
2 sticks Cinnamon
½ cup Water

Peel sweet potatoes or yams and slice in ½-inch rounds. In a bowl, mix brown sugar, flour and salt. In a 4-quart saucepan, place ⅓ of sliced sweet potatoes or yams and sprinkle with ⅓ of sugar mixture. Dot with 1 tbls. of butter. Then place leftover ⅔ of sweet potatoes or yams on top. Sprinkle rest of sugar mix. Dot with 2 tbls. butter. Stick cinnamon sticks into potatoes, pour in water. Bring to a boil, cover and lower heat to low. Simmer 45 minutes. Place potatoes in a bowl and pour liquid over them. Serve warm.

VEGETABLES

Yataklete Kilkil (Yäh täh Klātā Kēl Kēl)

THIS DISH is traditionally served as a main course during Lent, but it is a delicious and beautiful accompaniment to many main dishes. This recipe originated in Ethiopia and serves six (6).

- 6 small Potatoes
- 3 large Carrots (peel, cut in 2-inch pieces)
- ½ lb. fresh Green Beans (trim, cut in 2-inch pieces)
- ¼ cup Vegetable Oil
- 3 small Onions (peel, quarter and separate)
- 1 large Green Pepper (seeded and cut in strips)
- 2 Hot Chilies (chopped)
- 1 tbls. Garlic (chopped)
- 2 tsp. Ginger or Ginger Root
- 1 tsp. Salt
- ½ tsp. Black Pepper
- 6 Scallions (cut in 2-inch pieces)

Boil potatoes, carrots and string beans in a large sauce pan for 5 minutes. Drain and rinse with cold water.

In a 4- to 5-quart cooking casserole or dutch oven, place oil, onions, green pepper and chilies, cook 5 minutes at moderate heat (do not brown). Add garlic, ginger, salt, pepper and cook 2 minutes more. Then add drained potatoes, carrots and beans, plus scallions. Toss and coat all with oil mixture. Reduce heat to low. Partly cover. Cook 10 more minutes and serve warm.

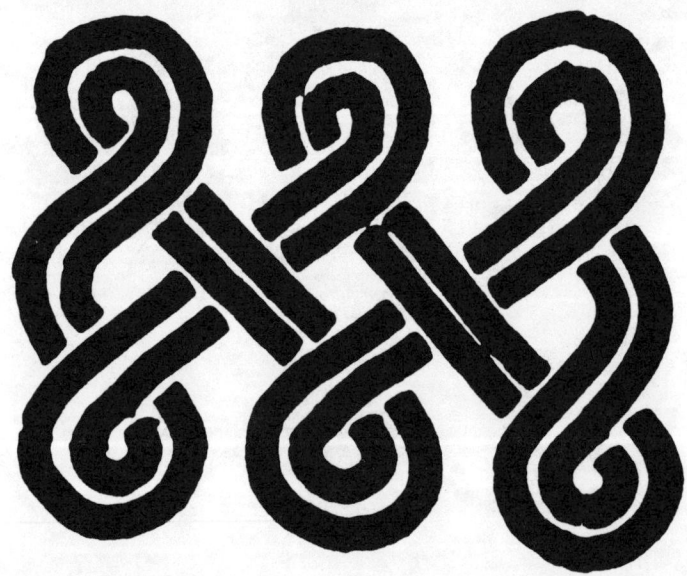

Side Dishes

Governor's Beans

SOME UNNAMED GOVERNOR at the Cape of Good Hope had a wonderful kitchen garden. He grew an enormous amount of spotted beans and served them often to men from the Dutch East India Trading Company. Thus, this became a famous South African dish. This recipe serves six (6).

- 1 12-oz. bag of Dried Pinto Beans
- 2 shoulder Lamb Chops
- 1 large 46-oz. can Tomato Juice
- 2 cups Water
- 1 tsp. Red Pepper
- ¼ tsp. Black Pepper
- 1 tsp. Salt
- 1 large Onion (chopped finely)
- 1 tbls. Peanut Oil

Put peanut oil and chopped onion in a large pot, sauté at moderate heat for 3 to 5 minutes. Place two lamb chops in the pot with the sautéed onion and brown on both sides. Turn off the heat and cool chops until they can be cubed and returned to the pot. Next add 2 cups water, 1 tsp. red pepper, black pepper and salt as well as the cubed meat. Bring all to a boil, turn down to moderate heat and cook covered for 10 minutes. At that time add the 12-oz. bag of dried pinto beans and the can of tomato juice. Cook all over low to moderate heat, mixing every 10 to 15 minutes until liquids are almost all absorbed and beans become soft and tasty.

SIDE DISHES

Geelrys

THIS *YELLOW RICE AND RAISINS* recipe was introduced to South Africa through French ancestry. The story goes: "A French Grandmother served this dish to her family in South Africa very often. After she died, the dish did not die with her. It was served from then on by her husband as a remembrance of all she had meant to him." This recipe serves four to six (4-6).

2 tbls. Butter
1 cup Long Grain Rice
2 cups Water
1 stick Cinnamon
1 tsp. Sugar
½ tsp. Turmeric
pinch Saffron
1 tsp. Salt
½ cup Raisins

Melt butter in a 3-quart saucepan and add rice. Coat rice with butter but do not brown. Add the water, cinnamon, turmeric, saffron and salt. Bring to a boil, cover and turn to low heat. Cook for 20 minutes until water is gone. Discard cinnamon and add raisins and sugar. Serve warm.

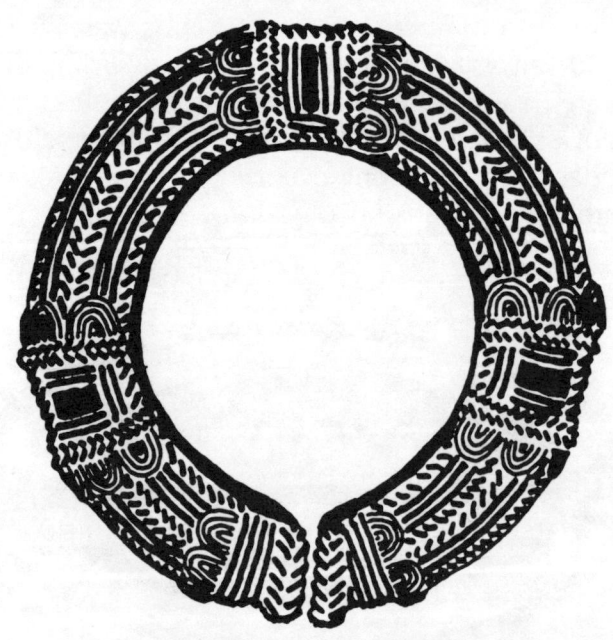

SIDE DISHES

Arroz de Coco (Arrōz Dā Cōcō)

MOZAMBIQUE WAS a famous slave trading place during the 19th Century as it is located in a Coastal Tropical Area. It is still well-known today for the coconut farming business, and coconut milk is used in many of their fine recipes such as the one below. This rice dish originated in Mozambique, South Africa and serves four (4).

- 2 tbls. Vegetable Oil
- ½ cup Onions (chopped finely)
- 1 small Green Pepper (chop finely)
- 1 cup uncooked Long Grain Rice
- 1 tsp. Salt
- 1½ cups Coconut Milk
  Can be made by: chopping 1½ cups Coconut and add to 1½ cups Hot Water
- 2 Tomatoes (chopped finely)
- 2 tsp. Chilies (chopped finely)

In a large skillet, heat the oil. Sauté onions and green pepper for 5 minutes over moderate heat. Add rice and cook for 3 minutes. Stir in coconut milk mixture, tomatoes and salt. Cover and simmer over low heat for 20 minutes. When all liquid is absorbed, remove pan from heat and stir in chilies. Cover and let set at room temperature for 10 minutes. Serve warm.

SIDE DISHES

Yemiser Salatta (Yā mē sāir Säh läh ttäh)

A VEGETARIAN LENTIL DINNER that originated in Ethiopia and serves four (4). Ethiopian Good Friday is celebrated as an observance of Easter. Dishes such as Yemiser Salatta are selected and served at the Lentil Feasts!

½ lb. Dried Lentils
4 tbls. Red Wine Vinegar
2 tbls. Vegetable Oil
1 tsp. Salt
¼ tsp. Black Pepper

8 large Shallots (peel, cut in half)
2 Hot Chilies (seed and cut in 1" strips)

Rinse lentils in a sieve. Boil in salted water (3" water over the lentils) for 30 minutes. Drain in a sieve and rinse with cold water. Drain thoroughly.

In a bowl, mix vinegar, oil and pepper. Add lentils, shallots, and chilies. Mix well. Marinate at room temperature for 30 minutes. Serve with bread and vegetables.

SIDE DISHES

Injera (ēn jā räh)

ETHIOPIAN BREAD IS another name for Injera which is a necessary supplement to many African meals, especially the Wats and the stews. Injera tastes faintly sour and very soothing. It is an excellent contrast to the hotly spiced dishes like the Wats. Most African families make enough Injera to last them 3 days (approx. 25 pieces per family).

Breads are also served in Africa with Milky Wild Honey. It is interesting to note that an Ethiopian delicacy would be to eat Injera covered with a slab of honey in the comb with young grubs in the comb.

¾ cup Buckwheat Flour
¾ cup All-purpose Flour
3 tsp. Baking Powder
1 cup Club Soda
½ tsp. Salt
1 Egg (beaten)
2 tbls. Butter (melted)

Mix flours, baking powder and salt in a bowl. Stir in egg and club soda until batter is creamy. Cook at once in a buttered skillet. Fry 2 tbls. batter for 1 to 2 minutes on one side only. Serve warm with or under main dishes. The club soda takes the place of a sour dough starter. (This is made in the same fashion as crepes in a pan.)

Desserts

Tanzanian Fruit Salad

FRESH FRUITS served alone or in a combination salad as below are the most typical ending to an African's meal. This recipe originated in East Africa and serves four (4).

- 2 cups Pineapple Cubes
- 4 heaping tbls. Grated Coconut
- 2 heaping tbls. Cashew Nuts
- 8 tbls. Light Cream
- 2 tbls. Honey
- 6 tbls. White Rum or Banana Liqueur

Mix pineapple, coconut and cashews together in a bowl. Add cream, honey and rum. Mix well and let stand 1 hour at room temperature. Refrigerate and serve cool.

DESSERTS

Steamed Papaya

THE PAPAYA is called a "tree melon" in Africa. They grow as small as pears and as large as 20 pounds. They are often eaten for breakfast, sprinkled with lime juice or as a dinner compliment as in the recipe below. This recipe originated in East Africa and serves four (4). It is excellent with duck, chicken and lamb.

1½ lbs. Underripe Papaya (peel, seed and cut in cubes)	4 tbls. Butter ½ tsp. Salt ⅛ tsp. Nutmeg

Pour water in bottom of steamer (enough so it is 1 inch away from cooking rack) and steam papaya cubes for 20 minutes. When the cubes are tender, drain in a colander. Then melt butter in skillet over moderate heat. Place papaya in skillet with nutmeg and salt and toss gently. Heat until warm and serve warm.

DESSERTS

Ovos Moles De Papaia (Ōvōs Mōlās Dā Päh päh ē äh)

PAPAYA AND EGG YOLK PUDDING. This recipe originated in Mozambique, South Africa and serves four (4). Eggs are used sparingly in many parts of Africa. In fact in some parts, there are still taboos associated with eggs. However, eggs are the "Symbol of Fertility," and the dessert below would likely be used for a special occasion. There is an Old Ghanian saying that expresses the Africans' view of the egg: "The sun, too, is but an egg which hatches great things."

1 Papaya (peel, seed and chop coarsely)
¼ cup Lemon Juice
¼ cup Water
4 whole Cloves
5 Egg Yolks
1 Stick Cinnamon
2 cups Sugar

Place papaya, lemon juice and water into a blender. Blend 30 seconds at high speed. Scrape sides of blender and blend again until mixture is a smooth puree. You may have to do in batches. Place puree in a 3-quart saucepan. Add sugar, cinnamon, and cloves and bring to a boil at high heat, stirring constantly. Cook until a candy thermometer reaches 230 degrees. Take from the heat and discard the spices.

In a deep large bowl, beat egg yolks until they thicken. As you are beating constantly, pour hot syrup into yolks slowly until all is blended. Put in dessert dishes and refrigerate two hours.

DESSERTS

Cocada Amarela (Cō cäh däh Äh mäh rā läh)

YELLOW COCONUT PUDDING that originated in Mozambique and serves eight (8). Again, the influence of the coconut farms of Mozambique are in evidence here.

2 cups Sugar	6 cups Water
4 whole Cloves	4 cups Grated Coconut
12 Egg Yolks	Ground Cinnamon

Combine the sugar, cloves and water in a 4 to 5 quart saucepan. Bring to a boil. Continue boiling and stir constantly until syrup reaches 230 degrees on a candy thermometer. Reduce heat to low, take out cloves and add coconut. Mix thoroughly and cook 10 minutes on low heat. Take off heat.

In a deep bowl, place 12 egg yolks. Beat them with an electric mixer for one minute. Stir in 1 cup of sugar, coconut mixture and then pour yolks into saucepan with rest of syrup. Cook at medium heat 10 minutes. Pour in 1-inch deep platter or individual dessert dishes. Sprinkle with cinnamon and refrigerate for 2 hours.

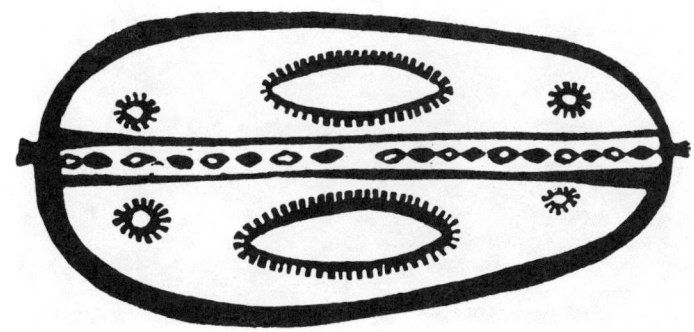

DESSERTS

Banana Fritters

THE WEST AFRICANS are known to be very innovative in their use of the banana and the plantain. This dessert surely shows this to be the truth. The beauty and taste of these fritters cannot be matched by any other heritage! Bananas are also sometimes sliced and served in a mayonnaise-lemon sauce, put into many custards, mixed in with the fufu recipes and made into an extraordinary Banana Wine. This recipe originated in West Africa and makes 20 delightful fritters.

1½ cups All-purpose Flour	4-5 medium Bananas
6 tbls. Sugar	Vegetable Oil for frying
3 Eggs	Powdered Sugar
¾ to 1 cup Milk	

Stir flour and sugar together (preferably with a whisk). Beat in eggs one at a time. Add milk, ⅓ cup at a time. Beat batter until smooth and elastic. It should stretch like a ribbon as you lift it out of the bowl. Peel bananas, chop coarsely and place in shallow bowl. Mash with table fork until pureed. Stir puree into batter. Let set 30 minutes.

Fry in 2-3 inches of oil at 375 degrees. Each fritter is about ¼ cup of batter. Turn once or twice. Fry until golden brown. Drain on paper towels and while still warm, sprinkle with powdered sugar.

DESSERTS

Koeksisters

SNAIL SHELL DOUGHNUTS. This recipe was introduced to the Capetown, South African people by the Malays. They were particularly great at pastries. This recipe is extremely delicious but a dieter's horror!

2 cups Flour	Syrup: 1½ cups Sugar
¼ tsp. Salt	⅓ cup Water
1 tsp. Baking Powder	Juice of 1 Lemon
3 tbls. Butter	½ tsp. Cinnamon
2 Eggs	1 tsp. Vanilla
Oil for frying	(Loose Sugar)

Sift flour, salt and baking powder into a large bowl. Cut butter into flour until it is like coarse sand. Mix in eggs and roll out dough on floured surface. Dust top of dough with flour. Cut small triangles. Roll up into snail shell shape by rolling it up around your finger. Fry each in oil until golden brown. Drain on paper towels.

Make syrup: Boil sugar, water, lemon juice, cinnamon and vanilla in saucepan until very syrupy.

Brush each fried snail shell with the syrup and then roll it in loose sugar.

DESSERTS

Krakelinge

SOUTH AFRICAN COOKIES. This pastry reflects Dutch ancestry. Cape cooking brought in the bisquits, pastries, cookies, etc. as a last accomplishment. As cookies became popular in South Africa, many were named after national events and historical facts. This recipe makes approximately 30 cookies.

- 1½ cups All-purpose Flour
- 1 tsp. Baking Powder
- ¼ lb. Butter (softened)
- 1 whole Egg (beaten)
- ½ cup peeled Almonds (ground)
- 1 tsp. Cinnamon
- ⅛ tsp. Salt
- ¾ cup Sugar
- 1 Egg White w/2 tsp. Water, beaten until frothy

Sift flour, baking powder, cinnamon and salt onto wax paper and set aside. In a bowl, cream 7 tbls. of butter and sugar and blend well. Beat in egg and then mix in flour mixture ½ cup at a time. With hands, knead dough into a ball. Roll out on floured surface to a 7" by 14" rectangle about ¼" thick.

Cut in 25 strips ½" wide by 7" long. Shape strips into a figure 8 and pinch closed. Grease cookie sheets with rest of butter. Place cookies on sheets and coat with beaten egg whites and ¼ cup sugar mixed with ground almonds. Bake at 400 degrees for 12 minutes until brown.

DESSERTS

Soetkoekies

WINE AND SPICE COOKIES. This recipe originated in Capetown, South Africa, however, its ancestry reveals the influence of the Dutch. The name Soetkoekies means "Sweet Cookie."

5 tbls. soft Butter	1¼ cups Dark Brown Sugar
2 cups All-purpose Flour	1 Egg (beaten)
1 tsp. Cinnamon	¼ cup Sherry or Port Wine
1 tsp. Baking Soda	½ cup chopped Almonds
¼ tsp. ground Cloves	15 whole peeled Almonds cut in half
¼ tsp. Salt	
½ tsp. Ginger	1 Egg White plus 2 tbls. Water beaten until frothy

Grease 2 large baking sheets with 1 tbls. butter. Sift flour, cinnamon, baking soda, cloves, salt and ginger onto wax paper and set aside. In a deep bowl, place 4 tbls. butter and brown sugar. Blend well. Beat in 1 egg and slowly blend in flour mixture. Then add wine and chopped almonds. Beat well. Knead dough, flour, and roll out on floured surface until ¼" thick. With cutter, cut 2" rounds, place on baking sheets. Top each round with half almond and brush with egg whites. Bake at 350 degrees for 15 minutes until crisp.

DESSERTS

Ginger Cookies

SIERRA LEONE. This recipe is popular in West Africa. Even though cookies are not traditionally West African, they have become increasingly popular since they were introduced many years ago by expatriates.

    2 cups sifted All-purpose Flour
    6 tbls. Sugar
    3 tsp. Ginger
    ½ tsp. Salt
    ⅛ tsp. ground Red Pepper
    6 tbls. Butter
    4 tbls. Milk

Sift dry ingredients into a bowl. Rub in the butter until you get the consistency of a pie dough. Then add liquid and mix into a firm dough. Roll out on a floured board to ⅜" thick. Cut into circles. Place on a greased cookie sheet and bake for 15 minutes at 350 degrees.

DESSERTS

Coconut Lemon Cookies

ANOTHER increasingly popular cookie recipe is from Ghana, Africa. This one uses a plentiful local product, the coconut. This recipe is very crisp and tender with a delicate flavor.

½ cup Butter or Margarine
½ cup Sugar
½ cup Grated Coconut
1 tsp. Lemon Juice
1 tsp. Grated Lemon Rind
1 Egg (beaten)

1¼ cups sifted All-purpose Flour
¼ tsp. Salt
1 tsp. Cream of Tartar
½ tsp. Soda

Cream the butter and sugar together thoroughly. Mix in the coconut, lemon juice and lemon rind. In a separate bowl, sift together the flour, salt, cream of tartar, and baking soda. Add the beaten egg to the creamed mixture and then mix in the dry ingredients a little at a time. Mix well, and it should become a soft smooth dough. Turn dough out onto a well-floured board and roll into a thin sheet of dough. Cut into rounds and any other shape you may desire. Bake on greased cookie sheets for 5 to 7 minutes at 425 degrees.

DESSERTS

Peanut Cookies

THIS RECIPE originated in Nigeria and makes about 2 dozen cookies. It uses the very commonly grown peanut in Africa.

- ¼ cup Butter or Margarine
- ⅔ cup Sugar
- 1 Egg (beaten)
- 1¼ cups sifted Flour
- ½ tsp. Salt
- ½ tsp. Baking Powder
- ½ tsp. Vanilla (optional)
- ½ cup shelled roasted Peanuts

Cream the butter and sugar together until well blended. Add beaten egg and mix thoroughly. In a separate bowl sift together the flour, salt, and baking powder and then add to the creamed mixture blending well. Add vanilla.

Spread the peanuts on a board and crush them coarsely with a rolling pin. Form the dough into a ball and set it on the crushed nuts. Then with a floured rolling pin, roll the dough into the nuts. Turn the dough so that the nuts are spread evenly into it. Roll out to ¼ inch thick. Cut into rounds. Bake on greased cookie sheet for 12 to 15 minutes at 375 degrees.

DESSERTS

Plantain Gingerbread

TWO FRESH bananas may take the place of the plantain in this recipe. This is one of the recipes that shows the Africans' ingenuity with bananas and plantains. It is basically an upside-down cake that originated in Liberia and is a fantastic dessert.

- ½ cup Sugar
- ½ cup Water
- 2 cups sliced Plantains or fresh firm Bananas
- 2⅓ cups All-Purpose Flour
- ½ tsp. Salt
- 1½ tsp. Soda
- 1 tsp. Ginger
- 1 tsp. Cinnamon
- ¼ tsp. Cloves
- ¼ tsp. Nutmeg
- 3 oz. Butter or Margarine
- 1 cup Molasses
- ⅔ cup boiling Water or 1 cup Sour Milk (make by placing 1 tsp. Vinegar into 1 cup milk)

Place the sugar and water into a saucepan, mix and bring to a boil over moderate heat, stirring constantly. Add the whole plantain to the boiling sugar syrup and cook for 5 minutes. Remove it, place it on a plate to drain and cool. Slice the plantain into coin shaped slices.

Butter a 9-inch square cake pan very heavily. Spread the plantain slices evenly over the bottom.

Sift all dry ingredients together into a large bowl. Then place the butter and molasses in another saucepan and bring to a boil over moderate heat. Remove from heat. Add this heated mixture slowly to the dry ingredients and beat vigorously. Pour this batter over the sliced plantain (or bananas). Bake for about 50 minutes at 350 degrees. Test middle of cake with a toothpick to see if it is done. No batter should stick to toothpick poked in middle top of cake.

Let pan stand 5 minutes on a rack, then loosen sides with a spatula and turn the cake upside down on a serving plate. This Gingerbread is delicious served warm or cooled and extra special with a generous topping of whipped cream.

DESSERTS

Cinnamon Cake

THIS *SIMPLE CAKE* was adapted from "A Ghana Cook Book for Schools." It is a tasty and simple dessert.

- 2 cups All-purpose Flour
- 2 tsp. Cinnamon
- ½ tsp. Ginger (ground)
- 1 tsp. Baking Powder
- ½ cup Milk
- ½ cup Sugar
- ½ cup Butter or Margarine
- 2 tbls. Orange Marmalade
- 2 Eggs

Sift together into a large bowl all dry ingredients including the spices. In a saucepan mix the sugar, butter and orange marmalade, cook at a low heat for 5 minutes, stirring constantly. *Do not* bring to a boil. Set aside to cool. Beat the eggs and slowly add them to the cooled mixture. Then add marmalade mixture to dry ingredients. Last, add the milk and mix well.

Bake in a greased 9-inch loaf pan or springform pan at 350 degrees for about 35 to 40 minutes. Toothpick test to make sure cake is done. Let cake cool in its pan for 5 minutes and then turn out onto a cake rack. For added taste, you may wish to dust this cake with powdered sugar.

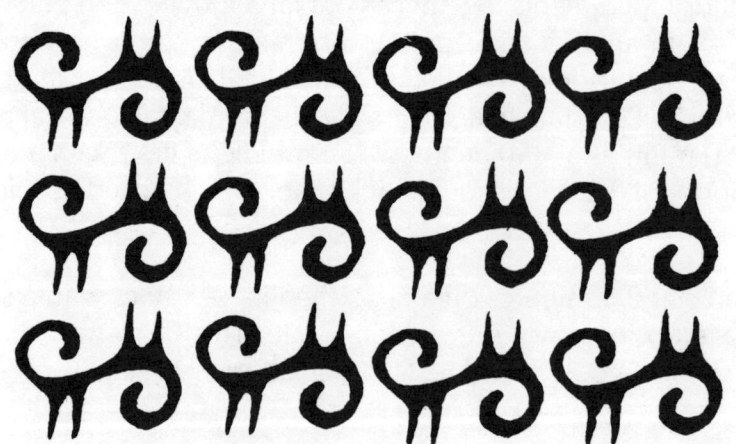

DESSERTS

Cornmeal Cake

CORN is not a native product of Africa as it was introduced by the Europeans. However, it is very widely used in Africa. This recipe originated in West Africa and is an interesting addition to this book. It is a type of African fruitcake.

1 cup Butter or Margarine
1 cup fine granulated Sugar
4 Eggs (beaten)
1 cup All-purpose Flour
1 cup Cornmeal (white)
¼ tsp. Allspice
Milk (as needed)

1 cup mixed Currants and White Raisins
1 cup Dark Seedless Raisins
½ cup chopped roasted Peanuts
¼ cup Brandy

Place butter and sugar together in a large bowl. Cream together until they are well-blended. Add the beaten eggs a little at a time until all is blended smoothly. In a separate bowl sift together the flour and cornmeal as well as the allspice. Add the dry ingredients to the egg mixture a little at a time until well blended. Next add the fruit and half of the chopped peanuts. Add the brandy and some milk if necessary. The mixture should be at a batter state where it drops softly off the end of your spoon.

Grease a 9-inch loaf pan or a 9-inch springform pan. Place the batter in it and bake at 325 degrees about 90 minutes or until it tests done with the toothpick test. Take out and let cool on a rack, then turn out, and it's ready to eat.

DESSERTS

Pineapple Pie

A RICH, DELICIOUS pie that originated in Liberia, West Africa. This recipe is tasty and light on a warm summer evening.

Pastry for a two-crust pie (you can make your own favorite crust or use any store brand)

- 2 Eggs
- 1 cup Sugar
- 1 tbls. Lime or Lemon Juice (fresh)
- 2½ cups Fresh Pineapple (crushed or grated)
- 1 tbls. Butter

Roll out on a floured surface one-half of the pastry crust and line an 8-9-inch pie plate with it. In a bowl, beat the eggs and sugar and lime or lemon juice until smooth. Blend the crushed or grated pineapple into this egg mixture and pour into the pastry shell.

Next roll out on a floured surface the other half of the pastry crust. Lay it over the top of the pie. Trim around the edge of the pie to get rid of any excess crust. Then go around the edge of the pie and press and flute the two crust edges together. Prick the top of the pie in several places with a fork.

Bake pie for 10 minutes at 425 degrees and then reduce the heat to 350 degrees and bake 35 minutes longer until the crust is lightly browned. Place on a rack to cool.

Suggestions

SPECIAL DINING PARTY IDEAS.

First, I must mention all the things that are characteristic of Africa, its people, and its foods. From this, you can pick what types of things you may want to purchase for a Special Dining Party; but you may want to start with the simplest and slowly purchase what you feel will be useful to you in the future, or what will add to your home decor permanently.

Africa is known for its beautiful hard woods—thus—wood carvings, wood masks, and possibly wood instruments such as the Bolo' are all beautiful wall decors for one's home. Wood serving bowls, especially for the Wats, the fruits, and for the ever popular "African bowl of steaming rice" are an excellent addition to your dining utensils. Simple wood serving trays and wood flat plates can be made out of 1" by 12" six foot board planks. Sawing a 1" by 12" pine board into six 1-foot pieces and sanding them smoothly could provide 6 wood dinner serving platters for around two dollars. It is interesting to note that in the peasant's hut in Africa, one may eat dinner on wood platters. Later in this chapter, I will introduce a Peasant Party with hors d'oeuvres as an introduction to a special dining party, using these simple wood platters.

Decor of the *most* importance in all African homes (no matter how poor) are the colorful woven baskets. Even the poorest of peasant homes will have at least one colorful woven basket. Covered baskets are used to serve the breads and fruits. It is not only colorful and decorative to serve food in these baskets, but it is also hygienic since it keeps the pesty flies off the food. An interesting idea for your home and table is to have at least one colorful covered basket to serve your breads, another basket for fresh fruits and an open colorful small basket for a table decoration. Instead of filling this basket to be used as a table decoration with traditional flowers or plants, collect and fill it with colorful feathers as would be used in Africa. Some feathers can be bought in stores while others you might find yourself. They can be collected on trips to the woods, beaches, etc., or you may have friends who farm or hunt and ask them to save some feathers for you from their fine feathered friends. Feathers and beads are widely used in Africa as body decorations and are a part of African tradition.

SUGGESTIONS

Africans do a lot of weaving with water rushes and grasses. Woven mats for your table or woven mats to sit upon can also add a bit of interesting decor to your dinner parties. Cloth weaving of mats, rugs, wall hangings, etc. is a major part of African tradition. Most woven cloths, mats and clothings are very colorful and have African geometric designs of all types. Adding a colorful geometric tablecloth to your table will create a stimulating base for a wonderful dinner.

No candlelight dinner for the African. Instead "oil lamps" will be used. Add a couple of oil lamps to your home inventory and fill them with the colorful oils sold locally. These lamps can romantically light your special dinner party as well as be handy around the house just in case the electricity goes out!

The serving dishes of Africa come in many forms and varieties. Very popular are the tin buckets, bowls, and plates as well as colorful earthenware bowls, plates and glasses. Clay pottery and clay bowls are also widely used and are handmade. The influence of North Africa brings us brassware of all types; and the African elite may even serve their foods and drink in crystal bowls, glassware, etc. Of course, the hard woods provide platters, bowls, etc. Hollow-dried gourds may also provide small serving bowls or drink containers. You now have several ideas of things you may want to add to your kitchen and dining area in order to create an African atmosphere.

The Art of Spices in Africa is two-fold. The aromatic odor of spices from cooking is used to stimulate the appetite, and the spices in the foods themselves are there to tantilize the tastebuds. Since spices are widely grown in Africa and a part of African tradition, it is simple and reasonable to use spices as an enhancement to your dinner meal. There, too, are many spice room deodorizers on the market nowadays; however, a unique way to fill the room with spiced aroma is with cheesecloth spice bags. I will later explain how you can spice up your dinner party.

A SUGGESTED DINNER PARTY

It is suggested that you first try a dinner party for eight (8). Ask that the dress be African—colorful head wraps of geometric design, loose flowing type clothing, dashikis for the men, and imaginative decorations of feathers and beads.

You set the scene by using the oil lamps with colorful oil both at the "Peasant Hors d'oeuvre Party" and at the dinner table. The shimmering lights of the oil lamps with low playing tribal drum music in the background, along

SUGGESTIONS

with the spiced aroma of food cooking in the kitchen will enhance the scene for a very special dining party.

A reasonable and easy way to scent the room with spices which entice the tastebuds is to buy cheesecloth and colorful ribbons. Cut several 6" by 6" squares of cheesecloth. Fill each square with various spices such as dried red peppers, bay leaves, cloves and stick cinnamon and tie each into a little bundle with colorful ribbons. These can be hung around the room, hung from chandeliers and even placed around the table decorations. Use them in any way your imagination can create.

We start our Special Dining Party with hors d'oeuvres served as a "Peasant Party." Weather permitting, this part of your dinner party could be set up outside on a stoop, patio, grassy area, etc., or on any floor in any room of your house or apartment. Cheap reed mats to sit upon are available at most import stores and similar to the reed sitting mats woven from river rushes by the Africans. An ahead-of-time preparation for this party would be to purchase 2 six foot pine boards 1" to 12". As stated previously, saw eight 1-foot pieces and sand thoroughly. Also sand the large leftover piece of plank. Each small board will become the lap platter for the hors d'oeuvre and the large plank can be used as the serving area and placed on the floor in the middle of the circle of reed mats. Place a colorful oil lamp and a couple of spice bags on the server. If you have the extra time with the board platters, using a wood burning tool, you can burn geometric African designs around the edges of the platters and the server. These boards can be used over again as they can be scrubbed and steel wooled for reuse.

The main hors d'oeuvre served in a peasant's hut would be snails collected live from a nearby stream, charcoaled over the hardwoods and served in a tin with a dish of palm-nut oil. If you wish to simulate this, you can purchase snails and snail shells and place the snails in the shells to be grilled over a hiabachi for a few minutes on each side over hot coals. Then place them into a tin or metal bowl to be passed around with a bowl of sauce made from 1 cup peanut oil (our palm-nut oil), 3 tbls. chopped parsley, 1 tsp. salt and ½ tsp. pepper. Also, serve a bowl of Samosas for those who cannot handle the likes of snails and if you have a group of raw meat lovers, a bowl of Kitfo with crackers and injera is also a very interesting hors d'oeuvre. Start this part of the party with a few of your favorite Bible passages and have soft tribal drum music playing in the background. This can be a time of conversation, getting acquainted, catching up on old times and having a drink or two. If you are in a large city area, you may even be able to purchase a bottle of Tedj, the African Liquor, which will warm up the tummy as well as the party . . . Then on to the main course.

SUGGESTIONS

A colorful geometric tablecloth enhances the main table. If your table is not too large it might be wise to set up a side serving table such as a card table and cover that also with a colorful geometric tablecloth. At any large material shop, a few yards of a heavy geometric material could be purchased and cut into tablecloths. It would not even be necessary to hem them as many woven African items are rough around the edges.

One or preferably two oil lamps with colorful oils provide the romantic lighting for one or both tables. Decorate the table(s) with a small colorful basket filled with feathers of all sizes and colors and have the bags of cheesecloth spices placed or hung in several parts of the room. Set your main table as you would for any dinner party; but as you need new items for your kitchen and dining area, consider going into colorful geometric dishes, earthenware glasses, clay pottery and wood serving bowls and casseroles. You will also find that the covered clay pottery used as a server helps the food hold its warmth throughout your complete dinner party. Also be sure to have a lovely covered basket on the main table with a napkin inside (preferably cloth) covering the Injera.

To serve the meal, the hostess places a large covered clay casserole loaded with Chicken Goober Stew along with a large wooden bowl of steaming rice and several small bowls of cut-up raw fruits and vegetables such as broccoli, cauliflower, pineapple, cantelope, strawberries, bananas, coconut, dry roasted peanuts or any variety of fruits and vegetables that you like and that are in season. At this time it is also worth mentioning that gourds are also very popular in Africa and if you have the time to properly dry them out and make little bowls out of them, it is extraordinarily unique to serve all the chopped fruits and vegetables in the gourds of various sizes and shapes and colors.

The rice is placed on the plates first and can be served by the hostess. The plate is then passed to the host who places the scoops of aromatic Chicken Goober stew on top of the rice. After every one has a filled plate, take turns passing all the beautiful and tasty fruits and vegetables and add a little of each to the top of the stew. It is like building a meal. You will be amazed at how delicious this unusual dinner is. Also, the vitamins and nutritional needs supplied by this dinner are the utmost. The taste and beauty of this dinner surpasses the artworks of the esteemed.

Later on, after the table is cleared and the palate has rested, you may want to end your dinner with a cup of coffee brewed strong and hearty and served with whipped cream and wild honey as well as the wonderful and tasty Koesisters. This makes a beautiful, delicious end to a wonderful dinner party.

SUGGESTIONS

OTHER DINNER SUGGESTIONS . . .

Appetizer	Snyssels Milk Soup
Dinner	Doro Wat Served with
	Yataklete KilKil
	Complemented with Injera & Berbere
Dessert	Tanzanian Fruit Salad

Appetizer	Avocado Smoked Fish
Dinner	Zanzibar Duck
	Red Cabbage and FuFu Dumplings
Dessert	Steamed Payaya

Appetizer	Fish-Shrimp Salad
Dinner	Bobotie and Injera
	Green Bean Atjar
Dessert	Banana Fritters

Appetizer	Curry-Beef Soup
Dinner	Meat Lagos
	Steamed Rice
	Yam or Sweet Potato Stew
Dessert	Cocada Amarela

Appetizer	Samosas
Dinner	Couscous
Dessert	Plantain Gingerbread

Or, use your imagination and put together a dinner that delights you and your own.
Enjoy an adventure in Black Heritage Cooking.

Acknowledgements—

Amarteifio, Dr. E., *A Recipe Book for Ghana Schools.*

Barnard, E., *The Kudeti Book of Yoruba Cookery.*

Bohannan, Paul, *Africa and Africans.* The Natural History Press, Garden City 1964. Rev. 1971.

Boyd, Andrew and P. Van Rensburg, *An Atlas to African Affairs.* Frederick Praeger, NY, 1965.

Chikote, Ronald H., *Portuguese Africa.* Prentice, 1967.

Dede, Alice, *Ghananian Favorite Dishes.* Accra: Anowvo, 1969.

Desmond, Judy, *Traditional Cookery of South Africa.*

Faull, Lesley, Braai and Barbeque and Meat on the Menu. Capetown: Books of Africa, 1967.

Gerber, Hild, *Cape Cooking, Old and New*—Traditional Cookery of Cape Malaya. Capetown: Bazkena, 1958.

Grigson, Jane, *The Art of Charcuterie.* Knopf, NY, 1968.

Jones, A.H.M. and E. Monroe, *A History of Ethiopia.* Oxford U. Press, 1968.

Kingsnorth, G.W. *Africa South of the Sahara.* Cambridge U. Press, 1966.

Renwick, Ethel H., *A World of Good Cooking.*

Sarakikya, Mrs. E. Pendaeli and Sister Agnesa Blaser, Recipe Book for Tanzania.

Slade, H.M., Mrs. Sladel's South African Cooking.

Sieff, Pamela, *South African Traditional Dishes.*

Vanderpost, Laurens, *Time-Life Books,* 1970.

Vanderpost, Laurens, *First Catch Your Eland,* Ulverscroft, Leicester, England, 1977-78.

Wilson, Ellen G., *A West African Cookbook.* M. Evans, 1971 and Flare Bks./Avon 1971.

Thanks to:
    South African Consul General Info. Ctr., Washington D.C.
    Rev. Tutterow for helping with the African name phonetics.
    Marilyn Burnson for helping me find the book for sources.
    My husband Bruce for making me keep at it and complete it.
    My pupils at 74th Street Elem. for causing the inspiration.